concert hall

*concert hall society
and concert hall
record club*

*discography
compiled by
john hunt*

Concert Hall discography

John Hunt

ISBN 978-1-901395-26-6

Travis & Emery Music Bookshop
17 Cecil Court
London
WC2N 4EZ
United Kingdom.
Tel. (+44) (0) 20 7240 2129.
newpublications@travis-and-emery.com

4

contents

Concert Hall: an introduction

As was the case with previous label discographies which I have compiled, my starting point for Concert Hall was the acquisition, through second-hand and some even more unusual outlets, of as many of the original discs as it was possible to find. The decade and a half following the LP becoming obselete was a veritable golden age for obsessive collectors. Not only were pristine examples of the records available at high prices through recognised dealers, but there was also a vast treasure trove to be found, at much more reasonable cost, in charity shops and flea markets.

However, whilst there is no substitute for actually listening to the records themselves, it obviously helps to have knowledge of a label's background and history, easily accessible in the case of established ones like Philips and Columbia but far more shadowy, as it turned out, in the case of the Concert Hall Record Club. And although in my earliest days as a collector I had been a member of the Club, receiving some of their LPs through the post, I had absolutely no knowledge of the background to these attractively priced recordings (one should not forget that in the early sixties the price of premium quality LPs from the major labels could be as much as two guineas, even forty-five shillings, if I remember correctly).

Concert Hall Society Inc. had been established in the United States in 1946 by the brothers David and Sam Josefowitz, who had arrived from Europe in 1938 to study chemistry and chemical engineering. However, it was David's passion for music which led them to conceive the idea of marketing limited editions of rare musical repertoire on a subscription basis, later also embracing sales through retail outlets. It seems that the first 78rpm record sets were manufactured from a vinylite material which made them lighter and easier to handle than the cumbersome shellac discs which were standard at the time. The recording sessions in and around New York, devoted to lesser known music from the seventeenth through to the twentieth centuries, gave much needed employment to the scores of Jewish refugee musicians who did not have the good fortune to be a Jascha Heifetz or an Artur Rubinstein.

It was probably the pressure felt from the major record companies Victor and Columbia that led the Josefowitz brothers to begin making their recordings in Europe, especially as they needed to employ larger forces for the standard orchestral repertoire which in the early fifties started to appear on a second label, known as the Musical Masterpiece Society. Family and business connections dictated that the first European destination was Switzerland, but soon a golden opportunity presented itself in the Netherlands, where a vast pool of orchestral musicians from the various municipal and radio organisations made themselves available, under pseudonyms such as Netherlands Philharmonic Orchestra, Concert Hall Symphony Orchestra and Handel Society Orchestra, to undertake a wide programme for Concert Hall

introduction/continued

in two Hilversum churches, the Hersteld Apostolische Kerk and Tessel-schadekerk. Later in the fifties recordings also started to be made for the label in Vienna, using players from the Staatsoper's pool of musicians (Wiener Philharmoniker in all but name!), who had already been working undercover, so to speak, for labels such as Vox, Vanguard, Nixa and Haydn Society (Concert Hall actually shared some recordings with these other companies).

By 1960 Concert Hall's American activities had been virtually abandoned, and with the label now circulating in the European territories mentioned above, as well as in France under the name of Guilde Internationale du Disque, it was time to enter the British market, albeit strictly as a record club rather than a retail label available through shops.

It has been suggested that Concert Hall owed some of its commercial success to the cutting of corners in basic recording techniques and manufacturing process, but I find the monophonic sound of its earlier productions no less acceptable than that of the big American record-makers of the time, rather dry to the European ear but otherwise natural in balance. One early publicity statement asserted that Concert Hall cut directly from masters, eliminating the mother and stamper discs used for mass production of commercial records. More disturbing was their introduction in 1956 of a programme of pre-recorded binaural stereophonic tapes, which apparently enjoyed only limited commercial success. Nonetheless, the process used for these reel-to-reel tapes formed the basis of the unfortunate synchro-stereo treatment applied to all Concert Hall LPs from the mid-sixties onwards: the original single-channel recording had its high frequency instruments (violins) channeled, apparently by means of a high-pass filter, to the left of the aural image, with the low frequency ones (cellos and double-basses) channeled to the right by means of a low-pass filter – artificial reverberation was then added to enhance the illusion of stereo separation. Decca also adopted the process to disfigure its perfectly acceptable mono back catalogue in re-issues on the Eclipse label, and EMI did the same for its early seventies re-issues of classic recordings from the fifties (Columbia operetta recordings with Elisabeth Schwarzkopf, operas with Maria Callas and even Herbert von Karajan's first Beethoven symphony cycle). I recall being amazed, when working in retail at the time, how so many record buyers believed that they were purchasing genuine stereophonic products! However, before I protest any further about electronic stereo, I must note that a more sophisticated version of the procedure, described as ambient mastering, is now being used to enhance early recordings for the CD market by very reputable companies like Pristine and Testament, and hopefully this can be applied in due course to items from the Concert Hall catalogue which because of their musical values are well deserving of further exposure.

introduction/continued

Concert Hall must be one of very few organisations not to have its actual recording ledgers preserved, making it doubly difficult to obtain an overall view of its activities in any chronological sequence. At Michael Gray's suggestion, therefore, I have indicated known publication dates for records in the earlier parts of the catalogue where recording dates are not available (nor are the archives of individual orchestras likely to yield the desired data, given a situation in which their players were working for Concert Hall outside of their main contracts, that is on an ad hoc basis).

Whilst visual presentation of the discs (cover design) was certainly comparable to a company like Decca, and whilst sleeve notes were provided by an array of reputable music writers (Mosco Carner, Robin Golding, Noel Goodwin, Julian Herbage, John Lade, Nicholas Maw, Walter Panofsky, Malcolm Rayment, Willi Reich, Stanley Sadie and John Warrack), many inconsistencies occurred in numbering of multiple sets of LPs as these came to be more in demand. For example, a set of two or more discs might sometimes have just one catalogue number, whilst re-issued items within an anthology would on occasion retain their original number. When entering the data at the point of a record's publication, I have indicated as many as possible of its re-issues both under the Concert Hall imprimatur and also by other record companies.

Once established in Europe, a considerable catalogue of non-classical material was built up, embracing popular, jazz, folk and ethnic. Spoken word recordings, some licensed from other companies, brought performances from Vienna's Burgtheater and the Comedie Francaise. This material, however, has not been included in the current discography, which concentrates almost exclusively on what we can describe as western classical music. In this area alone there is a wealth of material waiting to be rediscovered, notwithstanding my earlier caveats about recording quality.

Regarding the performers, we encounter many unfamiliar names as well as some who did not make so many recordings despite their cnsiderable reputations (pianist Lili Kraus and conductor Fritz Busch spring to mind). Then there are those conductors who worked long and hard to build up Concert Hall's catalogue, each producing extensive but still undervalued discographies (Otto Ackermann, Carl Bamberger, Pierre-Michel le Conte, Walter Goehr, Gianfranco Rivoli, Hans Swarowsky, Henry Swoboda, Heinz Wallberg and David Josefowitz himself, who continued conducting for the label long after his direct commercial involvement with it had ceased). Or artists still near the beginning of their international careers (Philippe Entremont, Friedrich Gulda, Lorin Maazel, Pierre Boulez and Moshe Atzmon). Nor must we overlook the significant group of instrumentalists who contributed to Concert Hall's concerto and chamber music lists (Louis Kaufman, Ricardo Odnoposoff and the Guilet and Pascal String Quartets). Perhaps the greatest introduction/concluded

seal of approval came from that group of established senior maestri who
accepted invitations to record for the label (Paul Kletzki, Josef Krips,
Igor Markevitch, Pierre Monteux, Charles Munch and Carl Schuricht).

A glance at the conductor's index on page 194 will reveal that the lion's share
of the conducting for Concert Hall was carried by Walter Goehr. In fact
Goehr's name may fall in the list of the most recorded of all classical artists.
It was therefore my great disappointment that both David Josefowitz and the
conductor's son, composer Alexander Goehr, failed to respond to my
requests for diary entries which might help date some of the many recordings.
My thanks for assistance goes primarily to Michael Gray, David Patmore
(whose article on the Concert Hall labels in the Winter 2000 issue of Classic
Record Collector gave extensive detail on their activities), John Baker, Rudolf
Bruil, Dennis Davis, John Hancock, Roderick Krüsemann, Tully Potter and
Neville Sumpter.

As for a personal recommendation from the several thousand recordings
preserved on the Concert Hall label, and worthy of further investigation,
I have listed the following titles together with the catalogue numbers under
which the known data can be found: Beethoven Fidelio (2120), Beethoven
Christus am Oelberge (2550), Bliss Piano Concerto (CHS 1167), Bruckner
Symphony No 7 (2394), Handel Messiah (2153), Mahler Symphony No 1
(2269), Mahler Symphony No 4 (2638), Monteverdi L'incoronazione di
Poppea (CHS 1184), Mozart scenes from Le nozze di Figaro (2586), Mozart
Mass in c minor K427 (2376), Offenbach Les contes d'Hoffmann (2108),
Schubert piano works (2251), Schumann Piano Concerto (2190), Stravinsky
Le sacre du printemps (2324), Music by the Strauss family (2134, 2186,
2271, 2383 and 2595), Verdi Rigoletto (2371), Vivaldi Il cimento concerti
(CH-AR and CHS 1064) and Wagner overtures and preludes (2093, 2147,
2246, 2362 and 2598).

John Hunt   2011

78rpm subscription series 1946-1949 (10" and 12" discs)

CH-A1   prokofiev string quartet no 2
recorded in new york and first published in october 1946
gordon string quartet
lp issues: CHC 8 and CHC 14

CH-A2   copland piano sonata
recorded in new york and first published in december 1946
leo smit, piano
lp issue: CHC 51

CH-A3   purcell suite from the gordion knot untied
recorded in new york and first published in march 1947
little symphony orchestra
daniel saidenberg, conductor
lp issue: CHC 22

CH-A4   barber capricorn concerto
recorded in new york and first published in april 1947
little symphony orchestra
daniel saidenberg, conductor
lp issue: CHS 1078

CH-A5   bowles sonata for two pianos
recorded in new york and first published in may 1947
gold and fizdale, pianos
lp issue: CHS 1089

CH-A6   stravinsky sonata for two pianos
recorded in new york and first published in may 1947
gold and fizdale, pianos
further 78rpm issue: amphion A6
lp issue: CHS 1089

CH-A7   brahms piano sonata no 1 & two chorale preludes
recorded in new york and first published in august 1947
ray lev, piano
lp issue: CHC 5

CH-A8   bartok string quartet no 4

recorded in new york and first published in august 1947
quatuor guilet
lp issues: CHC 9 and CM 89

CH-A9   recital of scottish songs by beethoven

recorded in new york and first published in february 1947
richard dyer-benett, tenor
instrumental ensemble
lp issue: CHC 13

CH-A10   debussy cello sonata

recorded in new york and first published in october 1947
raya garbousova, cello
artur balsam, piano
lp issue: CM 53
cd: pristine audio PACM 030

CH-A11   william schuman symphony for strings

recorded in new york and first published in october 1947
concert hall symphony orchestra
edgar schenkman, conductor
lp issue: CHS 1078

CH-AA   bartok violin sonata no 2 & roumanian dances

recorded in new york and first published in october 1947
tossy spivakovsky, violin
artur balsam, piano
lp issue: CHC 39
this recording was allocated the catalogue number CH-A12 but according to world's encyclopaedia of recorded music it was not published under that number

CH-AB   william schuman string quartet no 4

recorded in new york and first published in february 1948
gordon string quartet

CH-AC   prokofiev piano pieces for children

recorded in new york and first published in february 1947
ray lev, piano
lp issue: CHC 26

CH-AD   grieg cello sonata

recorded in new york and first published in february 1947
raya garbousova, cello
artur balsam, piano
lp issue: CHC 11

CH-AE   schubert string quartet no 10 d87

recorded in new york and first published in may 1947
quatour guilet
lp issue: CHC 7

CH-AG   recital of irish songs by beethoven

recorded in new york and first published in february 1947
richard dyer-benett, tenor
instrumental ensemble

CH-AH   vivaldi-bach concerto in d minor & j.e.bach fantasia and fugue in f

recorded in new york and first published in 1947
ray lev, piano
lp issue: CHC 12

CH-AI   schumann humoreske in b flat

recorded in new york and first published in august 1947
paul loyonnet, piano
lp issue: CHC 6

CH-AL   copland danzon cubano for two pianos

recorded in new york and first published in july 1947
leo smit and aaron copland, pianos
lp issue: CHC 51

CH-AM   tchaikovsky piano concerto no 2

recorded in los angeles and first published in june 1947
santa monica symphony orchestra
jacques rachmilovich, conductor
shura cherkassky, piano
lp issue: CHC 3

CH-AN   khachaturian violin concerto

recorded in los angeles and first published in december 1947
santa monica symphony orchestra
jacques rachmilovich, conductor
louis kaufman, violin
lp issue: CHC 2

CH-AO   delius violin sonata no 1

recorded in new york and first published in december 1948
louis kaufman, violin
daniel saidenberg, piano
lp issue: CHS 1062

CH-AP   tchaikovsky scherzo a la russe

recorded in new york and first published in may 1948
leo smit, piano

CH-AR   vivaldi le 4 stagioni/4 concerti from il cimento

recorded between 25-31 december 1947 in carnegie hall new york
concert hall chamber orchestra
henry swoboda, conductor
louis kaufman, violin
further 78rpm issue: amphion (france) A 1
lp issues: CHC 1, CHS 1001, RG 120 and CM 56
cd: naxos 8.110297-110298
incorrectly described by naxos as the first ever recording of the work;
 orchestra consisted of members of the new york philharmonic symphony

CH-B1   barber cello sonata

recorded in new york and first published in december 1947
raya garbousova, cello
erich-itor kahn, piano
lp issue: CHS 1092

CH-B2   hindemith string quartet no 4
recorded in new york and first published in december 1947
quatuor guilet
lp issue: CHS 1086

CH-B3   schubert piano sonata no 15 d840 and allegretto d915/
sonata completed by krenek
recorded in new york and first published in 1947
ray lev, piano
lp issue: CHS 1072

CH-B4   ravel sonata for violin and cello
recorded in new york and first published in april 1948
oscar shumsky, violin
bernard greenhouse, cello
lp issue: CHS 1123

CH-B5   recital of sonatas by scarlatti
recorded in new york and first published in february 1948
ralph kirkpatrick, harpsichord
lp issues: CHS 1070 and 2081

CH-B6   stravinsky concertino for string quartet
recorded in new york and first published in april 1948
gordon string quartet

CH-B7   weill four poems of walt whitman
recorded in new york and first published in may 1948
william horne, tenor
garner, piano

CH-B8   haydn sonata in g for flute and keyboard
recorded in new york and first published in july 1948
rene le roy, flute
paul loyonnet, piano
lp issue: CHS 1082

CH-B9   piano music by blitzstein, cowell, dello joio, foss and smit
recorded in new york and first published in october 1948

played by the composers

CH-B10   janacek concertino for piano, strings and wind
recorded in new york and first published in october 1948
chamber ensemble
rudolf firkusny, piano
lp issue: CHS 1076

CH-B11   milhaud four little symphonies
recorded in new york and first published in july 1948
concert hall chamber orchestra
darius milhaud, conductor
lp issues: CHS 1076, CM 108 and american decca DL 1956

CH-B12   dvorak string quartet no 4 in c
recorded in new york and first published in october 1948
gordon string quartet
lp issue: CHS 1075

CH-B13   dello joio trio for flute, cello and piano
recorded in new york and first published in july 1948
julius baker, flute
daniel saidenberg, cello
leonard hambro, piano

CH-B14   couperin suite du sixieme ordre
recorded in new york and first published in october 1948

paul loyonnet, piano

CH-B15   respighi violin sonata in b minor
recorded in new york and first published in july 1948
oscar shumsky, violin
artur balsam, piano

CH-C1   mendelssohn piano quartet no 2 in f minor
recorded in new york and first published in january 1949
quatuor guilet
artur balsam, piano
lp issue: CHS 1095

**CH-C2   monteverdi tirsi e clori, complete ballet and iro's
aria from il ritorno d'ulisse in patria**

recorded in basel and first published in january 1949
schola cantorum basilienses
august wenzinger, conductor
scherz-meister, soprano
max meili, tenor
lp issues CHS 1085 and nixa CLP 1085

CH-C3   randall thompson string quartet no 1

recorded in new york and first published in january 1949
quatuor guilet
lp issue: CHS 1092

CH-C4   brahms serenade no 1

recorded in new york and first published in october 1949
concert hall symphony orchestra
henry swoboda, conductor
lp issues: CHS 1087, nixa CLP 1087 and classic (france) 6094

CH-C6   bach fifteen 2-part inventions

recorded in new york and first published in october 1949
ralph kirkpatrick, harpsichord
lp issues: CHS 1088 and 163

CH-C7   recital of songs by charles ives
recorded between 24 may-2 june 1947 in new york
mcchesnay, tenor
herz, piano

CH-C8   mozart piano concerto no 13 in c k415

concert hall symphony orchestra
henry swoboda, conductor
artur balsam, piano
further 78rpm issue: amphion (france) A 3
lp issues CHC 31 and CHS 1116

CH-C9 **schubert quartet in g d96/**this is schubert's arrangement of a
guitar trio by matiegka
recording published in 1948
jaunet, flute
kertesz, viola
mottier, cello
leeb, guitar

CH-C10 **copland violin sonata & nocturne no 1**

recorded in new york and first published in september 1949
louis kaufman, violin
aaron copland, piano
lp issue: H 1640 (sonata)

CH-C11 **bloch piano sonata**

recorded in new york and first published in september 1949

ray lev, piano

CH-C12 **haydn concerto for violin, keyboard and orchestra**

concert hall chamber orchestra
henry swoboda, conductor
peter rybar, violin
hans andreae, harpsichord
further 78rpm issue: amphion (france) B3
lp issue: CHS 1081

CH-C13 **handel trio sonata in g op 5 no 4**

peter rybar, violin
anton fietz, viola
hans andreae, harpsichord

CH-C14 **richard strauss cello sonata**

raya garbousova, cello
erich-itor kahn, piano

concurrent 78rpm (prefix D) and 33.1/3rpm (prefix DL) series 1950-1952

CH-D1/DL 1   vivaldi concerto op 6 no 11 & sinfonias in c and f

concert hall chamber orchestra
henry swoboda, conductor
ales, violin

CH-D2/DL 2   dvorak piano quartet no 2 in e flat

recording first published in february 1950
artur balsam, piano
peter rybar, violin
otto kromer, viola
tusa, cello

CH-D3/DL 3   mozart symphonies no 14 k114 and no 24 k182

winterthur symphony orchestra
henry swoboda
other 78rpm issue: amphion (france) B 4 (symphony 14 only)

CH-D4/DL 4   bartok suite op 4

concert hall symphony orchestra
henry swoboda, conductor

CH-D5/DL 5   works by haydn
organ concerto in c
winterthur symphony orchestra
oskar kromer, conductor
k.matthäi, organ
divertimento in b flat (DL 5 only)
winterthur octet

CH-D6/DL 6   works by dello joio
three ricercari for piano and orchestra
concert hall symphony orchestra
henry swoboda, conductor
g.smadja, piano
three songs to english texts (DL 6 only)
j.druary, tenor
paul rogell, piano

CH-D7/DL 7   **mendelssohn string quartet no 4 in e minor**
quatuor guilet

CH-D8/DL 8   **recital of keyboard music by sweelinck, byrd and bull**
ralph kirkpatrick, harpsichord

CH-D9/DL 9   **martinu concerto for piano and double string orchestra**

concert hall symphony orchestra
henry swoboda, conductor
artur balsam, piano

CH-D10/DL 10   **bach concerto for keyboard, flute, violin and orchestra bwv 1044**
recording first published in 1950
string orchestra
aimee van de wiele, harpsichord
caratge, flute
merckel, violin

CH-D11/DL 11   **beethoven piano trios no 1 in e flat and no 8 in g**

artur balsam, piano
daniel guilet, violin
andre navarra, cello
trio no 8 was an arrangement of an earlier trio for flute, bassoon and piano

CH-D12/DL 12   **concerti by telemann**

concerto for three violins and orchestra
concert hall symphony orchestra
henry swoboda, conductor
louis kaufman, peter rybar and anton fietz, violins
concerto for viola and orchestra (DL 12 only)
string orchestra
otto kromer, viola

CH-D13/DL 13 **rossini wind quartets nos 2 and 5**

paris wind quartet
other 78rpm issue: amphion (france) A 5 (no 2 only)

CH-D14/DL 14   works by handel

concerto grosso in b flat op 6 no 7
concert hall symphony orchestra
henry swoboda, conductor
sonata for two oboes and keyboard (DL 14 only)
baudot and goubet, oboes
aimee van de wiele, harpsichord

CH-D15/DL 15   schubert string quartet in e d353 and quartettsatz d703
winterthur string quartet
d703 was on DL15 only

CH-D16/DL 16   quincy porter violin sonata in a minor

louis kaufman, violin
artur balsam, piano

CH-D17/DL 17   camargo guarnieri violin sonata no 2

louis kaufman, violin
artur balsam, piano

CH-D18/DL 18   kodaly summer evening and dances of marosszek
concert hall symphony orchestra
henry swoboda, conductor
dances of marosszek were on DL18 only

lp retail series CH-E, CH-F, CH-G and CH-H 1950-1952

CH-E1   mozart serenade no 7 k250 "haffner"
recorded between 31 august-9 september 1949 in the stadthaus winterthur
winterthur symphony orchestra
fritz busch, conductor
cd: guild GHCD 2352

CH-E2   concerti by vivaldi

recorded between 4-8 august 1950 in the ballroom of dolder hotel zürich

concerto for two violins and orchestra rv513
winterthur symphony orchestra
clemens dahinden, conductor
louis kaufman and peter rybar, violins
further issues: CM 84 and 948
cd: naxos 8.110297-110298
concerto for four violins and orchestra rv580
winterhur symphony orchestra
clemens dahinden, conductor
louis kaufman, peter rybar, anton fietz and g.piraccini, violins
concerto in g for cello and orchestra
winterthur symphony orchestra
clemens dahinden, conductor
m.cervera, cello

CH-E3   brahms serenade no 2

concert hall symphony orchestra
henry swoboda, conductor

CH-E4   hindemith string quartet no 3

quatuor pascal

CH-E5   buxtehude three cantatas

h.vonlanthen, soprano
max meili, tenor
h.reichel, organ

CH-E6   works by ravel

violin sonata
louis kaufman, violin
artur balsam, piano
further issue: 2076
trois poemes de mallarme
winterthur symphony orchestra
victor desarzens, conductor
e.benoit, soprano

CH-E7   beethoven egmont, incidental music to goethe's drama

winterthur symphony orchestra
walter goehr, conductor
m.flury, soprano
r.bichler, speaker

CH-E8   music by twentieth century american composers

barber violin concerto
concert hall symphony orchestra
walter goehr, conductor
louis kaufman, violin
further lp issues: CHS 1238, CHS 1253, H 1653 and 105
david diamond string quartet no 3
quatuor guilet

CH-E9   works by bach

orchestral suite no 1 bwv1066
winterthur symphony orchestra
henry swoboda
concerto for two keyboards and orchestra bwv1060
winterthur symphony orchestra
henry swoboda, conductor
h.andreae and t.sack, harpsichords

CH-E10   tchaikovsky orchestral suite no 3

west austrian radio orchestra
hans moltkau, conductor

CH-E11   telemann suite for flute and strings

chamber orchestra
thomas scherman, conductor
aurele nicolet, flute

CH-E12   works by martinu
la reve de cuisine, suite from the ballet
chamber ensemble
henry swoboda, conductor
sonata for two violins and piano & cinq pieces breves
louis kaufman and peter rybar, violins
pina pozzi, piano

CH-E13   works by mendelssohn
die schöne melusine, overture
recorded between 31 august-9 september 1949 in the stadthaus winterthur
winterthur symphony orchestra
fritz busch, conductor
further issue: CM 147
piano quartet no 1 in c minor
string trio
artur balsam, piano

CH-E14   schubert symphony no 6 d589
winterthur symphony orchestra
victor desarzens, conductor
further issue: 2280

CH-E15   alessandro scarlatti sinfonias nos 4 & 5 and concerti grossi nos 1 & 3
winterthur symphony orchestra
clemens dahinden, conductor

CH-E16   handel oboe concerti nos 2 and 3
winterthur symphony orchestra
henry swoboda, conductor
p.valentin, oboe

CH-E17   works by twentieth century composers
honegger concerto da camera for flute and cor anglais
winterthur symphony orchestra
victor desarzens, conductor
aurele nicolet, flute
egon parolari, cor anglais
henry barraud sonatina for violin and piano
a.reyes, violin
j.de menasce, piano
78rpm issue of the barraud sonatina on amphion (france) B 9

CH-E18   schumann drei fantasiestücke for cello and piano;
märchenerzählungen for violin, cello and piano
l.pascal, violin (märchenerzählungen)
a.vacellier, cello
ray lev, piano

CH-F1   **mozart symphonies nos 29 k201 and 34 k338**
concert hall symphony orchestra
henry swoboda, conductor

CH-F2   **gounod petite symphony in b and liszt tasso**
winterthur symphony orchestra
victor desarzens, conductor

CH-F4   **works by twentieth century composers**
copland piano concerto
rai roma orchestra
aaron copland, conductor
leo smit, piano
further lp issues: CHS 1238 and H 1638
bloch four episodes for chamber orchestra
zürich radio orchestra
thomas scherman, conductor
further issues: LE 16 and H 1638

CH-F5   **works by monteverdi**
il combattimento di tancredi e clorinda
zürich radio orchestra
walter goehr, conductor
dora abel, soprano
hugues cuenod, tenor
derrick olsen, baritone
sonata sopra sancta maria
winterthur symphony orchestra
zürich radio chorus
walter goehr, conductor
dora abel, soprano
further lp issue: 3008 (both works)

CH-F6   **schubert overture in the italian style d591 and**
16 deutsche tänze d783 arranged goehr
concert hall symphony orchestra
walter goehr, conductor
further issue: 91 (overture)

CH-F7   **works by gluck and haydn**
recording first published in 1952
winterthur symphony orchestra
clemens dahinden, conductor
gluck flute concerto in g and haydn divertimento for flute and strings
w.urfer, flute
haydn cello concerto in d
a.tusa, cello

CH-F8   **works by twentieth century english composers**
recording first published in 1952
britten variations on a theme of frank bridge
lausanne chamber orchestra
victor desarzens, conductor
further issue: CHS 1252
vaughan williams concerto accademico
zürich radio orchestra
clemens dahinden, conductor
louis kaufman, violin
further issues: CHS 1253 and H 1653

CH-F9   **schumann piano quartet in e flat**
recording first published in june 1952
ray lev, piano
daniel guilet, violin
w.schoen, viola
d.soyer, cello

CH-F10   **beethoven violin concerto,   arranged by the composer**
for piano and orchestra
winterthur symphony orchestra
clemens dahinden, conductor
artur balsam, piano
furher issues: CHS 1239 and H 1639
cd: bridge 9196

CH-F11   **dvorak symphony no 4 in d minor**
recording first published in june 1952
orchester der wiener staatsoper
henry swoboda, conductor

CH-F12   **bach cantata cantata no 118 "o jesu christ mein lebenslicht"**
and sinfonia from cantata no 42
winterthur symphony orchestra
zürich bach choir
bernhard henking, conductor

CH-F14   string quartets by paganini (in e) and arriaga (no 3)
recording first published in june 1952
quatuor guilet

CH-F15   richard strauss violin sonata in e
louis kaufman, violin
artur balsam, piano
prokofiev cello sonata no 2
raya garbousova, cello
stimer, piano

CH-F16   martinu toccata e due canzoni and roussel concerto
for orchestra
recording first published in june 1952
concert hall symphony orchestra
henry swoboda, conductor

CH-F17   concerti by eighteenth century composers
string orchestra
clemens dahinden, conductor
albinoni concerto for two oboes and strings
egon parolari and a.raoult, oboes
manfredini pastorale from sinfonia da chiesa
louis kaufman and anton fietz, violins
torelli violin concerto in e minor
louis kaufman, violin
vivaldi flute concerto in c minor
r.meylan, flute

CH-F18   sibelius pelleas and melisande, suite from the incidental
music;   weber abu hassan and euryanthe, overtures
recording first published in june 1952
winterthur symphony orchestra
clemens dahinden, conductor

CH-G1   beethoven the two romances for violin and orchestra
winterthur symphony orchestra
walter goehr, conductor
max rostal, violin
further issue: 917

CH-G2   dvorak symphony no 5 in f
netherlands philharmonic orchestra
walter goehr, conductor
further issues: CHS 1240 and 121

CH-G3   sinfonias by c.p.e, j.c and w.f bach
recording first published in august 1953
concert hall chamber orchestra
maurits van den berg, conductor
further issue: CHS 1251

CH-G4   lopatnikov divertimento and rosza serenade
recording first published in august 1953
la jolla festival orchestra
nikolai sokoloff, conductor

CH-G5   schumann cello concerto
utrecht symphony orchestra
paul hupperts, conductor
bernard michelin, cello
schumann three romances for oboe and piano
j.marx, oboe
i.rosenberg, piano

CH-G6   concerti by vivaldi
oboe concerti in d minor (op 8 no 9) and in f
winterthur symphony orchestra
clemens dahinden, conductor
egon parolari, oboe
concerto for two trumpets and orchestra
otto ackermann, conductor
f.hausdorfer and harry sevenstern, trumpets
further issues: CHS 1242 (d minor concerto) and 84 (d minor concerto)
cd: rediscovery (concerto for two trumpets)

CH-G7   tchaikovsky fatum, voyevode and elegy for strings
netherlands philharmonic orchestra
walter goehr, conductor
further issue: 66 (voyevode and elegy)

CH-G8   works by bartok
contrasts for violin, clarinet and piano
daniel guilet, violin
herbert tichman, clarinet
ruth budnevich, piano
further issue: 89
piano suite and allegro barbaro
frank pelleg, piano

CH-G9   debussy fantaisie pour piano et orchestre and faure masques et bergamasques
recording first published in september 1953
netherlands philharmonic orchestra
walter goehr, conductor
frank pelleg, piano (debussy)
further issues: 81 (debussy), 102 (faure) and RG 119 (faure)

CH-G10   mozart symphonies nos 17 K129 and 26 k184 and violin concerto k294a "adelaide"
netherlands philharmonic orchestra
otto ackermann, conductor
louis kaufman, violin
cd: modernio MR 001 (concerto)

CH-G11   hummel piano concerto in a minor and clementi sonata op 40
recording first published in september 1953
winterthur symphony orchestra
otto ackermann, conductor
artur balsam, piano
further issues: CHS 1241 and H 1641
cd: bridge 9196 (hummel), pristine audio PASC 201 (hummel) and pristine audio PAKM 006 (clementi)

CH-G12   works by berg and hindemith
recording first published in september 1953
berg sieben frühe lieder
zürich radio orchestra
walter goehr, conductor
kathryn harvey, soprano
further issue: LE 16
berg five pieces for clarinet and piano op 5
herbert tichman, clarinet
ruth budnevich, piano
further issue: LE 16
hindemith viola sonata op 11 no 4
tursi, viola
echaniz, piano

CH-G13   **paganini violin concerto no 2 in b minor**
utrecht symphony orchestra
paul hupperts, conductor
ricardo odnoposoff, violin
cd: doremi DHR 7874-7879
mendelssohn capriccio brillant for piano and orchestra
winterthur symphony orchestra
walter goehr, conductor
frank pelleg, piano

CH-G14   **works by eighteenth century composers**
walter goehr, conductor
haydn symphony no 46
netherlands philharmonic orchestra
further issue: CM 129
wondratscheck harpsichord concerto in f
zürich radio orchestra
frank pelleg, harpsichord

CH-G15   **works by bach**
violin concerto in g minor bwv 1056
winterthur symphony orchestra
clemens dahinden, conductor
peter rybar, violin
concerto for violin and oboe bwv 1060
winterthur symphony orchestra
clemens dahinden, conductor
peter rybar, violin
egon parolari, oboe
sonatas in c minor bwv1024 and b bwv1037
peter rybar and anton fietz, violins
t.sack, harpsichord

CH-G16   **works by de falla and kodaly**
recording first published in september 1953
de falla fantasia baetica
frank pelleg, harpsichord
kodaly string quartet no 2
quatuor hongrois

CH-H1 **beethoven musik zu einem ritterballett woO1**
and jena symphony, attributed to beethoven
netherlands philharmonic orchestra
walter goehr, conductor
further lp issues: 921 (ritterballett) and 2034 (jena)

CH-H2 **franck psyche, les eolides and le chasseur maudit**
netherlands philharmonic orchestra
walter goehr, conductor
further lp issues: CHS 1243, RG 119 (psyche) and 3004

CH-H3 **concerti by mozart**
winterthur symphony orchestra
horn concerto no 4
otto ackermann, conductor
j.zwagerman, horn
further issue: 87
bassoon concerto in b flat/spurious
otto ackermann, conductor
f.hollard, bassoon
organ sonata k328
walter reinhart, conductor
k.matthäi, organ

CH-H4 **works by britten and shostakovich**
simple symphony
concert hall symphony orchestra
otto ackermann, conductor
ovid metamorphoses
egon parolari, oboe
concerto no 1 for piano, trumpet and strings
concert hall symphony orchestra
walter goehr, conductor
noel mewton-wood, piano
harry sevenstern, trumpet
further issues: CHS 1252 (britten) and 205 (britten)
cd: pristine audio PASC 135 (shostakovich), british music society
BM 101 (shostakovich) and abc classics 4961 9002 (shostakovich)

CH-H5 **works by mendelssohn**
serenade and allegro for piano and orchestra
zürich tonhalle orchestra
otto ackermann, conductor
frank pelleg, piano
piano quartet no 3
winterthur string trio
frank pelleg, piano

CII-H6   chopin fantasy on polish airs
netherlands philharmonic orchestra
otto ackermann, conductor
hannes kann, piano
dvorak wind serenade op 44
netherlands philharmonic orchestra
otto ackermann, conductor

CH-H7   max reger clarinet quintet
winterthur string quartet
g.couteleu, clarinet
further lp issue: CHS 1244

CH-H8   music by haydn and boccherini
haydn symphony no 27 and violin concerto in g
concert hall symphony orchestra
walter goehr, conductor
j.skrypka, violin
boccherini symphony in a op 37 no 4
winterthur symphony orchestra
clemens dahinden, conductor

CH-H9   works by couperin, lully and leclair
couperin ballet suite
netherlands philharmonic orchestra
maurits van den berg, conductor
further issue: CHS 1523
lully ballet suite
netherlands philharmonic orchestra
walter goehr, conductor
leclair sonata for violin, cello and harpsichord
g.ciompi, violin
l.rostal, cello
h.chessid, harpsichord

CH-H10   tchaikovsky string quartet no 3
quatuor pascal

CH-H11   concerti by c.p.e.bach and stamitz
c.p.e.bach cello concerto
winterthur symphony orchestra
victor desarzens, conductor
a.tusa, cello
stamitz harpsichord concerto
winterthur symphony orchestra
clemens dahinden, conductor
frank pelleg, harpsichord

CH-H12 debussy violin sonata and piano music by dukas, goossens, malipiero, roussel and stravinsky
o.colbentson, violin
e.ulmer, piano
further issue: MMS 103 (debussy)

CH-H14 works by schubert
adagio d612 and scherzo from sonata d459
frank pelleg, piano
violin sonata in a d574
louis kaufman, violin
pina pozzi, piano

CH-H15 chamber music by hindemith and poulenc
hindemith sonata for viola d'amore
jan van helden, viola d'amore
j.huckriede, piano
further issue: CHS 1250
hindemith kleine kammermusik
netherlands philharmonic wind quintet
poulenc sextet for piano and wind
netherlands philharmonic wind quintet
h.krugt, piano

CH-H16 concerti by eighteenth century composers
vivaldi concerto in d minor for viola d'amore
netherlands philharmonic orchestra
otto ackermann, conductor
johann van helden, viola d'amore
further issue: 84
torelli concerto in forma di pastorale; marcello concerto grosso in f op 1 no 4; durante concerti no 5 in a and no 6 in a
netherlands philharmonic orchestra
maurits van den berg, conductor
further issue: 2080

CH-H17 grieg string quartet
quatuor pascal

CH-H18 twentieth century chamber music
bernstein clarinet sonata and milhaud clarinet sonatina
herbert tichman, clarinet
ruth budnevich, piano
bloch violin sonata no 1
louis kaufman, violin
pina pozzi, piano

handel society lp issues with prefix HDL 1952

HDL 1 (2-lp)   israel in egypt,   oratorio
handel society orchestra and chorus
walter goehr, conductor
elsie morison, soprano
marjorie thomas, contralto
richard lewis, tenor
further lp issue: classic (france) 6167-6168

HDL 2 (3-lp)   acis and galatea, opera
handel society orchestra and chorus
walter goehr, conductor
margaret ritchie, soprano
william herbert and richard lewis, tenors
trevor anthony, bass
further lp issue: classic (france) 6169-6171

HDL 3   three organ concerti arranged for harpsichord: no 13 in f; no 14 in a; no 15 in d minor
zürich radio orchestra
walter goehr, conductor
frank pelleg, harpsichord
further lp issue: classic (france) 6158

HDL 4   harpsichord suites nos 1, 2 and 3
frank pelleg, harpsichord
further lp issues: 2306 (suite 2) and classic (france) 6199

HDL 5   harpsichord suites nos 4, 5 and 6
frank pelleg, harpsichord
further lp issues: 2306 (suites 4&5) and classic (france) 6219

HDL 6   harpsichord suites nos 7 and 8
frank pelleg, harpsichord
further lp issue: 2306 (suite 7)

HDL 7   harpsichord suites nos 9, 10, 11 and 12
frank pelleg, harpsichord
further lp issue: classic (france) 6195

HDL 12 (3-lp)   judas maccabaeus, oratorio

utah symphony orchestra and university chorus
maurice abravanel, conductor
phyllis moffet, soprano
beryl jensen, contralto
william olvis and martin sorensen, tenors
marion hayes, bass

HDL 13 (2-lp)   alexander's feast, oratorio

handel society orchestra and cornell university chorus
robert hull, conductor
leona scheunemann, soprano
leslie chabay, tenor
keith falkner, bass
further lp issues: 2016 and classic (france) 6256-6257

HDL 14   apollo e dafne, italian cantata

zürich radio orchestra
walter goehr, conductor
kathryn harvey, soprano
derrick olsen, bass
further lp issue: classic (france) 6123

HDL 15 (2-lp)   saul, oratorio

orchestra, chorus and soloists of the crane department of music
brock mcelerhan, conductor
further lp issue: classic (france) 6206-6207

HDL 16 (2-lp)   johannes-passion

winterthur symphony orchestra
zürich bach choir
bernhard henking, conductor
kathryn harvey, soprano
gertrud pfenninger, contralto
ernst haefliger, tenor
derrick olsen, bass
further lp issue: classic (france) 6281-6282

HDL 17   chandos anthems nos 6 and 11

netherlands handel society orchestra and chorus
jack lorij, conductor
dora van doorn, soprano
annie woud, contralto
leo larsen, tenor
david hollestelle, bass
further lp issue: classic (france) 6191

HDL 18 (2-lp)   giulio cesare in egitto, opera

handel society orchestra and chorus
walter goehr, conductor
sylvia gähwiller and maria helbling, sopranos
friedrich brückner-rüggeberg, tenor
paul sandoz, baritone
siegfried tappolet, bass
further lp issues: 2032, classic (france) 6235-6236 and musical masterpiece society OP 29
excerpts from the recording appear on 5010 in set 5010-5022

HDL 19   italian cantatas: cecilia volgi un sguardo; dalla guerra amorosa

netherlands handel society orchestra
jack lorij, conductor
dora van doorn, soprano
leo larsen, tenor
david hollestelle, bass
further lp issue: classic (france) 6195

HDL 20   cantatas: salve regina; nel dolce dell' oblio

netherlands handel society orchestra
jack lorij, conductor
dora van doorn, soprano
dolce pur d'amor
instrumental ensemble
annie woud, contralto
spande ancor
netherlands handel society orchestra
jack lorij, conductor
david hollestelle, bass
further lp issue: classic (france) 6220

CHC lp series 1949-1951 (10" and 12" discs)

CHC 1 see CH-AR   **CHC 2** see CH-AN
CHC 3 see CH-AM

CHC 4   brahms clarinet quintet op 115
recording first published in 78rpm on the international label in april 1948
stuyvesant string quartet
gallodoro, clarinet
78rpm issue: international M 1303
further lp issues: classic (france) 6204 and nixa CLP 1004

CHC 5 see CH-A7   **CHC 6** see CH-AI
CHC 7 see CH-AE   **CHC 8** see CH-A1
CHC 9 see CH-A8

CHC 10   liszt six etudes d'apres paganini
recording first published in 78rpm on the international label in october 1947
robert goldsand, piano
78rpm issue: international M 306
further lp issue: CHS 1149

CHC 11 see CH-AD
CHC 12 see CH-AH
CHC 13 see CH-A9

CHC 14   hindemith ludus tonalis for piano
recording first published in august 1949
bruce simonds, piano
coupled with prokofiev second string quartet from CH-A1 and CHC 8

CHC 16   recital of piano music by faure
recording first published in may 1950
paul loyonnet, piano

CHC 17   beethoven violin sonata no 5 "spring"
recording first published in july 1949
joseph bernstein, violin
ella goldstein, piano

CHC 18   **haydn piano sonatas no 7 in c and no 11 in g**

recording first published in february 1950

lily dumont, piano

CHC 19   **villa-lobos string quartet no 6**
recording first published in 78rpm on the international label in august 1947
stuyvesant string quartet
78rpm issue: international M 301 and D 3001

CHC 20   **bloch string quartet no 2**

recording first published in 78rpm on the international label in january 1948
stuyvesant string quartet
78rpm issue: international M 302

CHC 21   **mozart symphony no 20 k133**
recording first published in 78rpm on the vox label in march 1947
vox chamber orchestra
edvard fendler, conductor
78rpm issues: vox 16009-16010 (set 171) and classic (france) 2065-2066

CHC 22   **purcell abdelazer suite**
little chamber orchestra
daniel saidenberg, conductor
coupled with purcell gordion knot untied suite from CH-A3

CHC 23   **schubert symphony no 1 d82**
recording first published in february 1950
winterthur symphony orchestra
henry swoboda
further lp issues: CHS 1080 and CM 2

CHC 25   **mozart piano sonata no 13 k333**

recording first published in february 1950

lily dumont, piano

CHC 26   **recital of piano music by tchaikovsky**
recording first published in august 1950
ray lev, piano
coupled with prokofiev piano pieces for children from CH-AC

CHC 27   **beethoven piano trio op 1 no 1**
recording first published in february 1950
members of the quatuor guilet
artur balsam, piano

CHC 28   brahms string sextet op 36

recording first published in march 1950

winterthur string sextet

CHC 29   corelli concerti grossi op 6 nos 2 and 3

recording first published in february 1950
concert hall string orchestra
henry swoboda, conductor

CHC 30   haydn symphonies nos 77 and 78

recording first published in february 1950
concert hall symphony orchestra
henry swoboda, conductor

CHC 31   see CH-C8

CHC 33   bach keyboard concerto bwv1053 and fugue bwv947

recording first published in march 1950
winterthur symphony orchestra
oskar kromer, conductor
hans andreae, harpsichord

CHC 36   french and italian madrigals

recording first published in february 1950

randolph singers

CHC 37   vivaldi sonatas in b flat and e minor arranged by d'indy

recording first published in february 1950
ricardo odnoposoff, violin
leo rostal, cello
benjamin oren, harpsichord
heinz wehrle, organ
cd: doremi DHR 7874-7879

CHC 38   schumann string quartet no 3

recording first published in may 1950

winterthur string quartet

CHC 39   see CH-AA

CHC 40   works by bach and vivaldi
recording first published in may 1950
bach violin concerto in a minor bwv1041 & vivaldi concerto op 3 no 6
concert hall ensemble
joseph bernstein, violin
vivaldi sonata in a for violin and keyboard
joseph bernstein, violin
r.starer, piano

CHC 41   arias from operas by pergolesi
recording first published in september 1950
ellen faull, soprano
peter rogell, piano

CHC 42   beethoven string quartet no 10 op 74 "harp"

recording first published in may 1950

winterthur string quartet

CHC 43   boccherini string quartets op 10 no 2 and op 33 no 5

recording first published in may 1950

quatuor guilet

CHC 44   choral music from the baroque era
recording first published in may 1950
dessoff choir
paul boepple, conductor
further issue: 2419

CHC 45   dvorak piano quintet in a
recording first published in may 1950
wintherthur string quartet
pina pozzi, piano
further issue: 154

CHC 46   brahms piano quintet op 34

recording first published in june 1950
winterthur string quartet
clara haskil, piano
further lp issue: nixa CLP 46

CHC 47   choral works by josquin and lassus
recording first published in july 1950
dessoff choir
paul boepple, conductor

CHC 48   songs by chinese composers
yi-kwei sze, bass
nancy lee sze, piano
further issue: CM 139

CHC 49   faure la bonne chanson, song cycle
recording first published in january 1951
j.brainard, soprano
j.paull, piano

CHC 50   flute concerti by boccherini and marcello
recording first published in june 1950
gothic string ensemble
paolo renzi, flute
further lp issue: nixa CLP 50

CHC 51   see CH-A2 and CH-AL

CHC 52   english and american madrigals and partsongs
recording first published in june 1950

randolph singers

CHC 53   schumann carnaval

recording first published in september 1950

f.sheridan piano

CHC 54   bach three sonatas for gamba and harpsichord
recording first published in june 1950
d.soyer, cello
h.chassid, harpsichord

CHC 55   franck prelude chorale & fugue; prelude fugue & variations
recording first published in november 1950
ray lev, piano
further issue: nixa CLP 55

CHC 56   vivaldi 3 flute concerti op 10; bassoon concerto in b flat
recording first published in november 1950
gothic string ensemble
paolo renzi, flute
bernard garfield, bassoon

CHC 57   folk airs of central and south america
mabel luce, mezzo-soprano
bocanegra and dalmar, guitars

CHC 58   violin works by contemporary composers
recording first published in may 1948
louis kaufman, violin
annette kaufman and theodore saidenberg, pianos

CHC 59   bach cantata no 78 "jesu der du meine seele"

recorded in may 1950 at a concert in schaffhausen for the international bach festival

winterthur symphony orchestra
winterthur and reinhart choirs
walter reinhart, conductor
ernst haefliger, tenor
hermann schey, bass
further issue: 70

CHC 60   bach magnificat in d bwv243

recorded in may 1950 at a concert in schaffhausen for the international bach festival

winterthur symphony orchestra
winterthur and reinhart choirs
walter reinhart, conductor
maria stader, soprano
else cavelti, contralto
ernst haefliger, tenor
hermann schey, bass
further issues: 31, nixa CLP 60 and classic (france) 6052

**CHC 61   schubert symphony no 5 d485 and mendelssohn
scherzo from the octet**
recorded between 31 august-9 september 1949 in the stadthaus winterthur
winterthur symphony orchestra
fritz busch, conductor
further lp issues: 20 (schubert) and nixa CLP 61
cd: guild GHCD 2352 (schubert)

*immediately after this point in the numerical sequence a change was made
over to prefix CHS and four-digit numbering as follows : -*

CHS lp series 1951-1955 (10" and 12" discs)

CHS 1062   violin sonatas by delius and robert russell bennett
louis kaufman, violin
theodore saidenberg, piano
delius sonata taken from CH-AO

CHS 1063 (2-lp)   beethoven die geschöpfe des prometheus, ballet
recording first published in january 1951
winterthur symphony orchestra
walter goehr, conductor
further issue: nixa CLP 1063

CHS 1064 (2-lp)   vivaldi seven concerti from op 8 nos 5-12
recorded between 4-8 august 1950 in the ballroom of dolder hotel zürich

winterthur symphony orchestra
clemens dahinden, conductor
louis kaufman, violin
further issue: 2063
cd issue: naxos 8.110297-110298
selection from the recording also issued on 104

CHS 1065   bruckner symphony no 3 in d minor/remington recording
recorded in salzburg and first published in march 1951
mozarteum orchestra salzburg
zoltan fekete, conductor
remington issue: 199-138
further issues: LPX 1047, concert artist LPA 1018, eurochord LPG 002 and
concerteum CR 223

CHS 1066   couperin viola da gamba suites nos 1 and 2
d.soyer, cello
h.chessid, harpsichord

CHS 1067   works by hindemith
recording first published in february 1951
concert hall symphony orchestra
walter goehr, conductor
konzertmusik for piano, brass and harp
artur balsam, piano
trauermusik for viola and orchestra
walter gerhart, viola

CHS 1068   arriaga string quartets nos 1 and 2
recording first published in january 1951
quatuor guilet
further issue: 1508

CHS 1069   dvorak suite for orchestra in d
recording first published in june 1951
winterthur symphony orchestra
henry swoboda
further lp issue: CHS 1157

CHS 1070   see CH-B5

CHS 1071   chausson concerto for violin, piano and string quartet
recording first published in june 1951
quatuor pascal
louis kaufman, violin
artur balsam, piano
cd: bridge 9225 and pristine audio PASC 049

CHS 1072   see CH-B3

CHS 1073   mozart flute concerto no 2 k314 and andante in c k315

recording first published in june 1951

winterthur symphony orchestra
henry swoboda, conductor
aurele nicolet, flute

CHS 1074   works by c.p.e.bach
recording first published in april 1951
keyboard concerto in d minor
winterthur symphony orchestra
victor desarzens, conductor
artur balsam, piano
cd: bridge 9196
trio sonata for clarinet, bassoon and keyboard
h.druart, clarinet
m.allard, bassoon
aimee van der wiele, harpsichord

CHS 1075   see CH-B12

CHS 1076   see CH-B10 and CH-B11

CHS 1077   concerti by c.p.e.bach and leopold mozart
recording first published in march 1951
winterthur symphony orchestra
clemens dahinden, conductor
c.p.e.bach flute concerto in g
aurele nicolet, flute
leopold mozart trumpet concerto
m.frei, trumpet

CHS 1078   see CH-A4 and CH-A11
CHS 1080   see CHC 23
CHS 1081   see CH-C12

CHS 1082   pergolesi flute concerto in g
recording first published in may 1951
winterthur symphony orchestra
clemens dahinden, conductor
r.meylan, flute
further lp issue: nixa CLP 1082
haydn flute sonata in g   see CH-B8

CHS 1083   mozart vesperae de dominica k321
recording first published in february 1951
winterthur symphony orchestra and chorus
walter reinhart, conductor
maria stader, soprano
lore fischer, contralto
ernst haefliger, tenor
hermann schey, bass

CHS 1084 (2-lp)   works by haydn and beethoven
recording first published in april 1951
haydn seven last words arranged for string quartet
quatuor guilet
beethoven elegischer gesang op 118
quatuor guilet
randolph singers

CHS 1085   see CH-C2
CHS 1086   see CH-B2
CHS 1087   see CH-C4
CHS 1088   see CH-C6
CHS 1089   see CH-A5 and CH-A6
CHS 1092   see CH-B1 and CH-C3

CHS 1093   **faure piano quartet no 2**
recording first published in july 1951
quatuor pascal
ray lev, piano
cd: pristine audio PACM 062

CHS 1095   see CH-C1

CHS 1100   **sacred choral music**
recording first published in july 1951
trapp family singers

CHS 1101   **at home with the trapp family singers**
recording first published in july 1951

CHS 1102   **schumann kreisleriana and novelette no 8**
recording first published in september 1951
ray lev, piano

CHS 1103 (2-lp)   milhaud service sacre
recording first published in june 1951
central synagogue choir
lazer weiner, conductor
a.richardson, organ
frederick lechner, baritone
m.wolfson, speaker

CHS 1104   **schumann davidsbündlertänze & arabeske**
recording first published in september 1951
ray lev, piano

CHS 1106   **rimsky-korsakov capriccio espagnol and
introduction and march from le coq d'or**
recording first published in june 1951
winterthur symphony orchestra
victor desarzens, conductor
further issues: RG 112 (coq d'or) and RG 113 (capriccio espagnol)
CHS 1107   **machaut messe de notre dame**
recording first published in june 1951
dessoff choir and brass ensemble
paul boepple, conductor

CHS 1108   **brahms variations and fugue on a theme of
handel and intermezzi op 117 nos 1 and 3**
recording first published in august 1951
lubka kolessa, piano

CHS 1109   **martin concerto for 7 wind & ibert flute concerto**
recording first published in august 1951
winterthur symphony orchestra
victor desarzens, conductor
peter lukas graf, flute
further issue: nixa CLP 1109

CHS 1110 (2-lp)   stainer the crucifixion, oratorio

recording first published in july 1951
whitehall choir
clifton helliwell, conductor
jan van der gucht, tenor
dennis noble, baritone
further issue: nixa CLP 1110

CHS 1111   **schumann etudes symphoniques and toccata**

recording first published in august 1951

lubka kolessa

CHS 1112   **choral works by perotinus magnus**
recording first published in january 1952
dessoff choir
paul boepple, conductor

CHS 1113   **brahms violin concerto op 77**
west austrian radio orchestra
hans moltkau, conductor
peter rybar, violin
further issues: 2007 and nixa CLP 1113
also issued on lp by classics club

CHS 1114   **schubert die schöne müllerin, song cycle**
recording first published in november 1951
martial singher, baritone
paul ulanowsky, piano

CHS 1116   see CH-C8

CHS 1117   **dvorak piano trio no 3 in f minor**
recording first published in february 1952
artur balsam, piano
louis kaufman, violin
marcel cervera, cello
further issues: classic (france) 6248 and classics club X 69

CHS 1118   norman dello joio a psalm of david
recording first published in february 1952
state university teachers' college orchestra
crane college choir
helen hosmer, conductor

CHS 1119   mozart piano concerti k37 and k39
recording first published in december 1951
winterthur symphony orchestra
walter goehr, conductor
artur balsam, piano

CHS 1120   mozart piano concerti k238 and k246
recording first published in december 1951
concert hall symphony orchestra
henry swoboda, conductor
artur balsam, piano
further issues: classic (france) 6083 and nixa CLP 1120
cd: bridge 9196 (k246)

CHS 1121   tchaikovsky orchestral suite no 1
winterthur symphony orchestra
walter goehr, conductor
further issue: nixa CLP 1121

CHS 1122   tchaikovsky orchestral suite no 2
recording first published in july 1952
winterthur symphony orchestra
walter goehr, conductor
further issue: nixa CLP 1122

CHS 1123   chamber music by ravel
string quartet
recording first published in 78rpm in june 1948 on the odeon label
quatuor pascal
78rpm issue: odeon 123 885-123 888
further issues: 2076 and classic (france) 6192
sonata for violin and cello   see CH-B4

**CHS 1124   song cycles by ravel: histoires naturelles, chansons
madecasses and chants populaires**
recording first published in november 1951
martial singher, baritone
paul ulanowsky, piano

CHS 1125   tchaikovsky piano concerto no 2
recording first published in april 1952
winterthur symphony orchestra
walter goehr, conductor
noel mewton-wood, piano
further issues: 131, 2070 and nixa CLP 1125
cd: pristine audio PASC 121 and abc classics 461 9002

CHS 1126   tchaikovsky piano concerto no 3 & concert fantasy in g
recording first published in january 1952
winterthur symphony orchestra
walter goehr, conductor
noel mewton-wood, piano
further issues: 186 (concert fantasy), 2070 (concerto) & nixa CLP 1126
cd: pristine audio PASC 126

CHS 1127   mendelssohn piano concerto no 1 and variations serieuses
netherlands philharmonic orchestra
walter goehr, conductor
frank pelleg, piano
further issues: 30 (both works) and 2059 (concerto)

CHS 1128   schumann violin concerto
recorded in 1951 in lausanne
lausanne symphony orchestra
victor desarzens, conductor
peter rybar, violin
further issues: 65 and nixa CLP 1128

CHS 1130   mozart string quartets nos 19 k465 and 21 k575
recording first published in march 1952
quatuor guilet
further issue: 122

CHS 1131 (2-lp)   verdi messa da requiem
recording first published in february 1952
calvary church choir
jack ossewaarde, conductor
l.hunt, soprano
j.moudry, contralto
p.knowles, tenor
k.smith, bass
further issue: nixa CLP 1131
according to world's encyclopedia of recorded music this version is played with organ accompaniment; the recording was also published in the usa in 1956 as a pre-recorded binaural stereophnic tape

CHS 1132   chopin etudes op 10 and trois nouvelles etudes
recording first published in april 1952
robert goldsand, piano
further issues: 158, 175 and nixa CLP 1132

**CHS 1133   chopin etudes op 25 & variations on herold's
je vends des scapulaires**
recording first published in april 1952
robert goldsand, piano
further issues: 101 (op 25), 175 (op 25) and nixa CLP 1133

CHS 1134 (2-lp)   vivaldi 12 concerti op 9 "la cetra"
recording first published in may 1952
strings of orchestre national de l'ortf
louis kaufman, violin and director

CHS 1135   beethoven christus am ölberge, oratorio
recording first published in may 1952
orchester der wiener staatsoper
wiener akademiechor
henry swoboda, conductor
margit opawski, soprano
radko delorco, tenor
walter berry, bass
further issue: nixa CLP 1135

CHS 1136   verdi quattro pezzi sacri
recording first published in may 1952
orchester der wiener staatsoper
wiener akademiechor
henry swoboda, conductor
further issue: classic (france) 6153
te deum and stabat mater only issued also on 2038

CHS 1137   works by edward macdowell
recording first published in april 1952
piano concerto no 2
orchester der wiener staatsoper
henry swoboda, conductor
alexander jenner, piano
cd: rediscovery (usa)
woodland sketches for solo piano
artur balsam, piano

CHS 1138   goldmark rustic wedding symphony
recording first published in may 1952
orchester der wiener staatsoper
henry swoboda, conductor
further issue: 49

CHS 1139   tchaikovsky symphony no 3 "polish"
recording first published in june 1952
orchester der wiener staatsoper
henry swoboda, conductor
further issue: nixa CLP 1139

CHS 1140   carpenter adventures in a perambulator
recording first published in may 1952
orchester der wiener staatsoper
henry swoboda, conductor
violin pieces by american composers
louis kaufman, violin
further issue: H 1640 and 132

CHS 1141   orchestral works by dvorak: nocturne for strings;
amid nature overture; carnival overture; othello overture
recording first published in april 1952
orchester der wiener staatsoper
henry swoboda, conductor
further issue: 42 (carnival overture)

CHS 1142   bruckner symphony in d minor "nullte"
recording first published in july 1952
concert hall symphony orchestra
henk spruit, conductor
further issues: classic (france) 6225 and nixa CLP 1142

CHS 1143   lalo violin concerto in f and schubert rondo in a
recording first published in july 1952
orchester der wiener staatsoper
henry swoboda, conductor
m.solovieff, violin
further issue: CHS 1176 (schubert)

CHS 1144   tchaikovsky orchestral suite no 3
recording first published in july 1952
winterthur symphony orchestra
walter goehr, conductor
further issue: nixa CLP 1144

CHS 1145   franck grande piece symphonique and liszt variations on bach's weinen klagen
recording first published in november 1952
eduard nies-berger, organ
further issue: nixa CLP 1145

CHS 1146   schubert impromptus d899 and d935
recording first published in september 1952
robert goldsand, piano
further issues: 2082 (d899) and nixa CLP 1146

CHS 1147   brahms paganini variations and schumann piano sonata no 2
recording first published in september 1952
robert goldsand, piano
further issue: nixa CLP 1147

CHS 1148   schubert sonata in a d664 and moments musicaux d780

recording first published in september 1952
robert goldsand, piano
further issues: 2083 and nixa CLP 1148

CHS 1149   piano music by liszt and rachmaninov
rachmaninov variations on a theme of chopin
recording first published in december 1952
robert goldsand, piano
liszt six etudes d'apres paganini   see CHC 10

CHS 1150   chopin piano sonata no 1 and variations on a german theme
recording first published in october 1952
robert goldsand, piano
further issues: H 1650 and nixa CLP 1150

CHS 1151   works by twentieth century composers
recording first published in september 1952
concert hall chamber orchestra
robert hull, conductor
vaughan williams flos campi
corenell a cappella choir
francis tursi, viola
hunter johnson letter to the world
j.fitzpatrick, piano
further issues: H 1651 and nixa CLP 1151 (both works)

CHS 1152   schubert string quartet in d minor d810 "der tod und das mädchen"
recording first published in march 1953
quatuor hongrois
further issues: 128 and nixa CLP 1152

CHS 1153   chopin piano concerto no 1 in e minor
recorded in hilversum and first published in march 1953
netherlands philharmonic orchestra
walter goehr, conductor
noel mewton-wood, piano
further issues: 35 and nixa CLP 1153
cd: dante HPC 015

CHS 1154   elgar enigma variations and serenade for strings
recorded in hilversum and first published in november 1952
concert hall symphony orchestra
walter goehr, conductor
further lp issue: nixa CLP 1154

CHS 1155   massenet le cid, ballet music from the opera and rimsky-korsakov tsar sultan, suite from the opera
recorded in hilversum and first published in november 1952
netherlands philharmonic orchestra
henk spruit, conductor
further issues: 911 (massenet), 2288 and nixa CLP 1155

CHS 1156   a classical recital on the saxophone: works by corelli, handel, purcell and kreisler
recording first published in march 1953
sigurd rascher, saxophone

CHS 1157   works by dvorak
suite for orchestra   see CHS 1069
string quartet in f "american"
recording first published in april 1953
quatuor hongrois
further issue: 185

CHS 1158   beethoven die ruinen von athen, incidental music
recorded in hilversum and first published in december 1952
netherlands philharmonic orchestra and chorus
walter goehr, conductor
annie woud, contralto
david hollestelle, bass
further issues: 2085 (overture) and nixa CLP 1158

CHS 1159   mendelssohn die erste walpurgisnacht
recorded in hilversum and first published in january 1953
netherlands philharmonic orchestra and chorus
otto ackermann, conductor
catharina hessels, contralto
cornelius kalkman, tenor
david hollestelle, baritone
further issue: 106

CHS 1160   concerti by twentieth century composers
recording first published in january 1953
prokofiev violin concerto no 1
zürich radio orchestra
heinrich hollreiser, conductor
ricardo odnoposoff, violin
further issues: 61 and nixa CLP 1160
cd: doremi DHR 7874-7879
stravinsky concerto for piano and winds
residentieorkest den haag
walter goehr, conductor
noel mewton-wood, piano
further issues: 64 , classic (france) 6151 and nixa CLP 1160
cd: british music society BMS 101

CHS 1161   a classical recital on the harmonica: works
by mozart, vivaldi, purcell and bach
recording first published in may 1953
larry adler, harmonica

CHS 1162   works for cello and orchestra

recording first published in january 1953
utrecht symphony orchestra
bernard michelin, cello
lalo cello concerto in d minor
toon verheij, conductor
faure elegie for cello and orchestra
paul hupperts, conductor

CHS 1163   mozart piano concerti in d k40 and in g k41
recording first published in january 1953
winterthur symphony orchestra
otto ackermann, conductor
artur balsam, piano
further issues: 925 (k41) and 943 (k40)

CHS 1164   **mozart three concerti k107, after j.c.bach**
recording first published in january 1953
winterthur symphony orchestra
otto ackermann, conductor
artur balsam, piano

CHS 1165   **symphonies by mozart: no 1 in e flat k16;
no 2 in b flat k17; no 5 in b flat k22; no 6 in f k43**
recording first published in january 1953
winterthur symphony orchestra
otto ackermann, conductor
further issues: H 1665 and classic (france) 6201

CHS 1166   **symphonies by mozart: no 4 in d k19; no 10 in g k74;
no 11 in d k84; no 14 in a k114**
recording first published in january 1953
winterthur symphony orchestra
otto ackermann, conductor
further issues: 99 (no 14 only),   H 1666, 3022 and classic (france) 6218

CHS 1167   **bliss piano concerto in b flat**

recording first published in january 1953
utrecht symphony orchestra
walter goehr, conductor
noel mewton-wood, piano
further issue: nixa CLP 1167
cd: pristine audio PASC 153 and british music society BM 101

CHS 1168   **a classical recital on the harmonica: works by
albeniz, bartok, enesco and granados**
recording first published in may 1953
larry adler, harmonica
l.colin, piano
bartok rumanian dances also issued on french mercury MLP 7026

CHS 1169   **a classical recital on the harmonica: works by bizet,
faure, lavry, rachmaninov and stravinsky**
larry adler, harmonica
l.colin, piano
further issue: 137

CHS 1170   **violin works by tartini, vitali and geminiani**
recording first published in march 1953
ricardo odnoposoff, violin
hans wehrle, organ (vitali)
hans wehrle, harpsichord (tartini)
further issue: 2080 (vitali and geminiani)

CHS 1172   mendelssohn string quintets op 18 and op 87

recording first published in may 1953
quatuor pascal
walter gerhard, viola
further issue: classic (france) 6239

CHS 1173   schumann piano sonata no 3 and intermezzi op 4

recording first published in june 1953
grant johannesen, piano
further issue: nixa CLP 1173
cd: pristine audio PAKM 009

CHS 1174   violin works by eighteenth century composers

recording first published in may 1953
max rostal, violin
tartini violin concerto in g minor
winterthur symphony orchestra
walter goehr, conductor
bach sonata for violin, cello and harpsichord bwv1023
a.tusa, cello
frank pelleg, harpsichord
biber passacaglia for unaccompanied violin
further lp issue: classic (france) 6187 (all works)

CHS 1175   music for violin and piano by de falla, nin and ysaye

recording first published in november 1954
ricardo odnoposoff, violin
jean antonietti, piano

CHS 1176   works by schubert
wanderer fantasy arranged by liszt for piano and orchestra
recorded in hilversum and first published in july 1953
netherlands philharmonic orchestra
walter goehr, conductor
grant johannesen, piano
twelve ländler d790
grant johannesen, piano
rondo in a for violin and orchestra   see CHS 1143

CHS 1177 symphonies by mozart: no 7 in d k45; no 8 in d k48; no 9 in c k73; no 12 in g k110
recorded on 10-11 december 1952 in hilversum
netherlands philharmonic orchestra
otto ackermann, conductor
further issues: H 1677, classic (france) 6243, discophilia DIS 15 and
otto-ackermann-archiv OAA 101

CHS 1178 symphonies by mozart: no 3 in e flat k18*; no 13 in f k112; no 15 in g k124; no 16 in c k128
recorded on 10-11 december 1952 in hilversum
netherlands philharmonic orchestra
otto ackermann, conductor
further issues: H 1678, classic (france) 6253, discophilia DIS 15
(symphonies 3 & 13) and otto-ackermann-archiv
OAA 101 (symphonies 3 & 13)
*symphony no 3 now known to be a composition by karl friedrich abel

CHS 1179 works by saint-saens
recording first published in june 1953
piano concerto no 3
winterthur symphony orchestra
victor desarzens, conductor
pina pozzi, piano
le carnaval des animaux
netherlands philharmonic orchestra
walter goehr, conductor
jean antonietti and isja rossican, pianos
further issues: 153 (carnaval), RG 129 and 2886 (carnaval)

CHS 1180 works by saint-saens
recording first published in june 1953
walter goehr, conductor
symphony no 2 in a minor
netherlands philharmonic orchestra
cello concerto in a minor
zürich tonhalle orchestra
paul tortelier, cello

CHS 1181 faure ballade for piano and orchestra
recording first published in july 1954
netherlands philharmonic orchestra
walter goehr, conductor
grant johannesen, piano
further issues: 102 and nixa CLP 1181
solo piano works by faure and poulenc
grant johannesen, piano
further issue: nixa CLP 1181

CHS 1182   franck string quartet in d
recording first published in october 1953
quatuor pascal
further issue: nixa CLP 1182

CHS 1183   tchaikovsky string quartet no 1 and glazunov 5 novelettes
quatuor hongrois

CHS 1184 (3-lp)   monteverdi l'incoronazione di poppea
recording first published in june 1953
zürich tonhalle orchestra and chorus
walter goehr, conductor
sylvia gähwiller, soprano
heidi juon, soprano
maria helbling, mezzo-soprano
friedrich brückner-rüggerberg, tenor
franz kelch, bass
further issue: classic (france) 6240-6242
excerpts also published on CHS 1226, 2028, 2807, 5010 in set 5010-5022 and OP 5
this was an edition prepared by walter goehr and was the first recorded performance of the work

CHS 1185   mozart string quintets k174 and k515
recording first published in august 1953
quatuor pascal
walter gerhard, viola
further issues: 3014 and classic (france) 6233

CHS 1186   mozart string quintets k406 and k516
recording first published in july 1953
quatuor pascal
walter gerhard, viola
further issues: 3015 and classic (france) 6234

CHS 1187   mozart string quintets k593 and k614
recording first published in july 1953
quatuor pascal
walter gerhard, viola
further issues: 3016 and classic (france) 6229

CHS 1188   mozart string quintets k46 and k407
recording first published in august 1953
quatuor pascal
walter gerhard, viola
werner speth, horn (k407)
further issues: 3017 and classic (france) 6237

CHS 1189   works by twentieth century composers

recording first published in february 1954
rochester chamber orchestra
robert hull, conductor
hunter johnson piano concerto
j.kirkpatrick, piano
honegger symphony no 2

CHS 1190   works by twentieth century composers
recording first published in january 1955
robert hull, conductor
vaughan williams fantasia on the old 104 th & three folksongs
rochester chamber orchestra
cornell a cappella choir
john hunt, piano
robert palmer chamber concerto
rochester chamber orchestra
m.taylor, violin
r.sprenkle, oboe
robert palmer slow slow fresh fount, after ben johnson
cornell a cappella choir

CHS 1191   christmas music and carols
don cossack choir
serge jaroff, conductor

CHS 1192   russian easter music
don cossack choir
serge jaroff, conductor

**CHS 1193   symphonies by mozart: no 18 in f k130;
no 19 in e flat k132; no 20 in d k133; no 21 in a k134**
recorded in hilversum and first published in may 1954
netherlands philharmonic orchestra
otto ackermann, conductor
further issue: H 1693

**CHS 1194   symphonies by mozart: no 22 in c k162;
no 23 in d k181; no 24 in b flat k182; no 25 in g minor k183**
recorded in hilversum and first published in may 1954
netherlands philharmonic orchestra
otto ackermann, conductor
further issues: H 1694 and 200 (symphonies nos 22 and 24)

CHS 1195   bruckner symphony no 3 in d minor
recorded in hilversum and first published in february 1954
netherlands philharmonic orchestra
walter goehr, conductor
further issue: 2018

CHS 1196   lassus domine ne in furore and monteverdi missa a 4 voci
recorded in hilversum and first published in february 1954
amsterdam motet choir
felix de nobel, conductor
further issue: classic (france) 6280

CHS 1197   moszowski piano concerto in e
recorded in hilversum and first published in january 1954
netherlands philharmonic orchestra
walter goehr, conductor
hannes kann, piano
further issue: classic (france) 6255

CHS 1198   favourite christmas carols on the organ

recorded in the mormon tabernacle salt lake city
alexander schreiner, organ
further issue: 38

CHS 1199   beethoven bagatelles op 33, op 119 and op 126
recording first published in april 1954
grant johannesen, piano
further issues: 919 (op 33 only), classic (france) 6273 and nixa CLP 1199

CHS 1201   beethoven string quartets op 18 no 1 and op 2 no 2 /
op 2 no 2 is an arrangement of piano sonata no 3
recording first published in november 1952
quatuor pascal
further issues: 2041 (op 18 no 1), nixa CLP 1201 (op 18 no 1) and
classic (france) 6249

CHS 1202   beethoven string quartets op 18 nos 2 and 3
recording first published in october 1952
quatuor pascal
further issues: 2041 (op 18 no 2), 2042 (op 18 no 3), classic (france) 6155
and nixa CLP 1202

CHS 1203   beethoven string quartets op 18 nos 4 and 5
recording first published in november 1952
quatuor pascal
further issues: 2042 (op 18 no 4), 2043 (op 18 no 5), classic (france) 6250
and nixa CLP 1203

CHS 1204   **beethoven string quartets op 18 no 6 and op 95**
recording first published in october 1952
quatuor pascal
further issues: 2043 (op 18 no 6), 2046 (op 95), classic (france) 6213
(op 18 no 6) and nixa CLP 1204

CHS 1205   **beethoven string quartet op 59 no 1**
recording first published in december 1951
quatuor pascal
further issues: 2044, classic (france) 6088 and nixa CLP 1205

CHS 1206   **beethoven string quartet op 59 no 2**
recording first published in december 1951
quatuor pascal
further issues: 2045, classic (france) 6117 and nixa CLP 1206

CHS 1207   **beethoven string quartet op 59 no 3**
recording first published in december 1951
quatuor pascal
further issues: 2045, classic (france) 6085 and nixa CLP 1207

CHS 1208   **beethoven string quartet op 74**
recording first published in november 1952
quatuor pascal
further issues: 2046, classic (france) 6146 and nixa CLP 1208

CHS 1209   **beethoven string quartet op 127**
recording first published in may 1951
quatuor pascal
further issues: 2047, classic (france) 6051 and nixa CLP 1209

CHS 1210   **beethoven string quartet op 130**
recording first published in may 1951
quatuor pascal
further issues: 2048, classic (france) 6058 and nixa CLP 1210

CHS 1211   **beethoven string quartet op 131**
recording first published in december 1951
quatuor pascal
further issues: 2049, classic (france) 6118 and nixa CLP 1211

CHS 1212   **beethoven string quartet op 135 and grosse fuge**
recording first published in april 1952
quatuor pascal
further issues: 2047 (op 135), 2048 (grosse fuge), classic (france)
6064 and nixa CLP 1212

CHS 1213   beethoven string quartet op 132
recording first published in november 1952
quatuor pascal
further issues: 2050, classic (france) 6227 and nixa CLP 1213

CHS 1214   beethoven string quintet in c op 29
recording first published in november 1952
quatuor pascal
walter gerhard, viola
further issues: 48, LE 1, 6232 in set 6227-6232 and nixa CLP 1214

CHS 1215   beethoven three piano quartets op posth
recording first published in january 1953
trio pascal
artur balsam, piano
further issues: 2054 and classic (france) 6208

CHS 1216   beethoven piano sonata no 14 arranged for string
quartet & sextet in e flat for string quartet and two horns
recording first published in april 1952
quatuor pascal
werner speth and carl rawyler, horns
further issue: classic (france) 6238

CHS 1217   beethoven string quintet in e flat op 4
recording first published in april 1952
quatuor pascal
walter gerhard, viola
further issue: classic (france) 6251

CHS 1225   music in shakespeare's time
recording first published in february 1955

susan bloch, virginals and lute

CHS 1226   see CHS 1184

CHS 1227   dittersdorf symphony in e flat and symphony
"the rescue of andromeda by perseus"
recording first published in july 1954
winterthur symphony orchestra
radio zürich orchestra
clemens dahinden, conductor

CHS 1229   **works by stravinsky**
recording first published in december 1954
danses concertantes and dumbarton oaks concerto
rochester chamber orchestra
robert hull, conductor
three pieces for string quartet
gordon string quartet

CHS 1230   **favourite encores**
don cossack choir
serge jaroff, conductor
further issue: 133

CHS 1231   **palestrina stabat mater and assumpta est maria**
recording first published in february 1956
dessoff choir
paul boepple, conductor
further issue: 2420

CHS 1234 (2-lp)   bach mass in b minor bwv232
recording first published in september 1956
orchester der bayerischen staatsoper
münchener lehrergesangverein
günther ramin, conductor
uta graf, soprano
herta töpper, contralto
gert lutze, tenor
max proebstl, bass
further issue: 2021

CHS 1237   schubert symphony no 9 d944 "great"
recorded in 1951 in de doelen utrecht
utrecht symphony orchestra
ignace neumark, conductor
further issues: 2023 and audio fidelity FCS 50058

CHS 1238 see CH-E8 and CH-F4   **CHS 1239** see CH-F10
CHS 1240 see CH-G2   **CHS 1241** see CH-G11

CHS 1242 see CH-G6   **CHS 1243** see CH-H2

CHS 1244 see CH-H7

CHS 1245 (2-lp)   handel messiah, oratorio
recording first published in may 1955
handel society orchestra and chorus
walter goehr, conductor
adrienne cole, soprano
watty krap, contralto
leo larsen, tenor
guus hoekman, bass
further issues: 2019 and OP 14
excerpts from the recording also on 522

CHS 1247   gershwin scenes from porgy and bess
recording first published in march 1956
opera society orchestra and chorus
paul belanger, conductor
margaret tynes, soprano
miriam burton, mezzo-soprano
joseph crawford, baritone
broc peters, bass
further issue: 2035

CHS 1249   rachmaninov preludes, selection

recording first published in march 1956

robert goldsand, piano

CHS 1250   sonatas by hindemith
sonata for viola d'amore and piano   see CH-H15
sonatas for clarinet and piano and for trumpet and piano
j.d'hondt, clarinet
harry sevenstern, trumpet
h.duval, piano

CHS 1251   see CH-G3
CHS 1252   see CH-F8 and CH-H4
CHS 1253   see CH-E8 and CH-F8

CHS 1254   concerti by vivaldi
recording first published in september 1956
concert hall symphony orchestra
otto ackermann, conductor
concerto for viola d'amore and strings
johan van helden, viola d'amore
two concerti for bassoon and strings
arnold swillens, bassoon
further issue: 5215-5216 (bassoon concerto in c)

CHS 1255 (3-lp) bach matthäus-passion
recorded in hilversum and first published in july 1956
rotterdam chamber orchestra
amsterdam oratorio and vredesholm boys choirs
piet van egmond, conductor
corry bijster, soprano
annie delorie, contralto
willy van hese, tenor
carel willink, bass
further issue: 2037
excerpts from the recording also on 3059

**CHS 1256   symphonies by mozart: no 17 k129; no 26 k184;
no 27 k199; no 28 k200**
recorded in hilversum and first published in august 1956
netherlands philharmonic orchestra
otto ackermann, conductor
further issues: H 1656 and 23 (no 17)

CHS 1257   symphonies by mozart: nos 30 k202 & 31 k297b
recorded in hilversum and first published in august 1956
netherlands philharmonic orchestra
otto ackermann, conductor
further issues: H 1657, RG 116, 200 (no 31) & 229 (nos 30 and 31)
symphony no 29 k201
orchester der wiener staatsoper
henry swoboda, conductor
further issues: H 1657 and 75
symphony no 32 k318
netherlands philharmonic orchestra
carl bamberger, conductor
further issues: H 1657 and 5003

CHS 1258   mozart symphonies no 33 k319 and no 37 k444
recording first published in august 1956
netherlands philharmonic orchestra
walter goehr, conductor
symphony no 34 k338
orchester der wiener staatsoper
henry swoboda, conductor
further issues: H 1658 (both) and 65 (no 34)

CHS 1259   mozart symphony no 36 k425 "linz"
recording first published in august 1956
winterthur symphony orchestra
walter goehr, conductor
further issues: H 1659 and 1
symphony no 39 k543
netherlands philharmonic orchestra
otto ackermann, conductor
further issues: H 1659, 2062 and 2145

**CHS 1260   symphonies by mozart: no 38 k504 "prague"
and no 41 k551 "jupiter"**
recorded in hilversum and first published in august 1956
netherlands philharmonic orchestra
otto ackermann, conductor
further issues: H 1660, RG 116 (no 41), 23 (no 41), 2061 (no 38)
and 2145 (no 38)

*CHS 1401   chopin the four ballades
this edition first published in october 1951
earl wild, piano

*CHS 1405   mozart piano concerto k451 and variations k354
this edition first published in october 1951
winterthur symphony orchestra
walter goehr, conductor
artur balsam, piano

*CHS 1410   mussorgsky pictures from an exhibition
this edition first published in october 1951
ella goldstein, piano

*no reason could be found for this out of sequence numbering

CHS lp series taken from the russian melodiya catalogue

CHS 1300   khachaturian violin concerto
this edition first published in june 1953
moscow radio orchestra
aram khachaturian, conductor
leonid kogan, violin
melodiya issue: D 0548-0549
other issue: chant du monde LDA 8051
cd: brilliant classics 93030

CHS 1301 (2-lp) tchaikovsky the snow maiden, complete incidental music for ostrovsky's drama
this edition first published in july 1953
bolshoi theatre orchestra and chorus
alexander gauk, conductor
zara dolukhanova, contralto
a.orfenov, tenor
other issues: monitor MEL 702-703 & chant du monde LDXA 8054
cd: brilliant classics 8866

CHS 1302   works by nineteenth century russian composers
this edition first published in september 1953
nikolai golovanov, conductor
glazunov symphony no 5
moscow radio orchestra
melodiya issue: D 0387-0388
dargomitzky what does this mean?/roussalka
bolshoi theatre orchestra
georg nelepp, tenor
mark reizen, bass
melodiya 78rpm issue: 017799-01802
melodiya lp issue: D 00831-00832
other issues: monitor MWL 337 and colosseum CRLP 139

CHS 1303   beethoven violin concerto
this edition first published in august 1953
moscow radio orchestra
alexander gauk, conductor
david oistrakh, violin
melodiya 78rpm issue: 01920-01941
melodiya lp issue: D 0498-0499
other issues: H 1603, 2017 and 2825
cd: dante LYS 331-334 and rca/bmg GD 69055
also issued by colosseum, bruno, eurodisc, fidelio, musidisc, period, vox and whitehall; 2825 was also issued in a 6-lp set of beethoven concerti but retaining original catalogue number and incorrectly naming conductor as kyrill kondrashin

CHS 1304   ballet music by prokofiev
this edition first published in may 1954
alexander stassevitch, conductor
cinderella, second suite from the ballet
bolshoi theatre orchestra
romeo and juliet, third suite from the ballet
moscow radio orchestra
other issues: monitor MWL 307 and chant du monde LDX 8073

CHS 1305 (3-lp)   tchaikovsky pique dame
this edition first published in april 1954
bolshoi theatre orchestra and chorus
alexander melik-pashayev, conductor
eugenia smolenskaya, soprano
eugenia verbitskaya, mezzo-soprano
georg nelepp, tenor
andrei ivanov, baritone
pavel lisitsian, baritone
melodiya issues: D 05558-05565 and D 05158-05163
other issues: monitor MWL 323-325 and artia MK 207
cd: arlecchino ARL 142-144, dante LYS 459-461 and preiser 90470
excerpts from the recording also on 2012 and OP 7

CHS 1306   chamber music by russian composers
this edition first published in july 1954
david oistrakh, violin
sviatoslav knushevitzky, cello
lev oborin, piano
glinka trio pathetique in d minor
other issues: monitor MC 2068 and colosseum CRLP 104
rimsky-korsakov piano trio in c
melodiya issues: D 04524-04525 and D 05542-05543
other issues: monitor MWL 317 and westminster WGM 8321
cd: chant du monde LDC 278907 and preiser 90595

CHS 1307 (3-lp) rimsky-korsakov sadko
this edition first published in april 1954
bolshoi theatre orchestra and chorus
nikolai golovanov, conductor
elisaveta shumskaya, soprano
vera davidova, mezzo-soprano
georg nelepp and ivan koslovsky, tenors
pavel lititsian, baritone
mark reizen, bass
melodiya issues: D 01480-01487 and M10 01480 01
cd: arlecchino ARL 23-25, dante LYS 316-318 and preiser 90655
also issued by ultraphon, monarch and chant du monde

CHS 1308   tchaikovsky manfred symphony
recorded on 6 december 1949 and this edition first published in september 1954
bolshoi theatre orchestra
alexander gauk, conductor
melodiya issue: D 2287-2290
other issue: monitor MWL 336
cd: brilliant classics 9146

CHS 1309   rachmaninov aleko, opera in one act
this edition first published in may 1954
bolshoi theatre orchestra and chorus
nikolai golovanov, conductor
nina pokrovskaya, soprano
a.orfonov, tenor
ivan petrov, baritone
melodiya issue: D 015-018
cd: arlecchino ARL 146-147

CHS 1310   (3-lp) tchaikovsky mazeppa
this edition first published in november 1954
bolshoi theatre orchestra and chorus
vassily nebolsin, conductor
nina pokrovskaya, soprano
vera davidova, mezzo-soprano
g.bolshakov, tenor
andrei ivanov, baritone
ivan petrov, bass
melodiya 78rpm issue: 019525-019526/019633-019670
melodiya lp issue: D 01286-01293/014757-014762
further issue: discocorp IGI 376
cd: dante LYS 266-268, preiser 90522, cantus classics 500481,
voci della luna VL 2019 and aquarius AQVR 175

CHS 1311   piano music by russian composers
emil gilels, piano/*recorded 1950-1951 in moscow*
glazunov piano sonata in f minor
melodiya lp issue: SM 04331-04332
cd: naxos 81.12051
also issued by colosseum, eurodisc, chant du monde & american columbia
prokofiev piano sonata no 2 in d minor
melodiya 78rpm issue: D 492-493
melodiya lp issue: SM 04403-04404
cd: naxos 81.12051
also issued by colosseum, bruno, chant du monde and artia
tchaikovsky piano pieces nos 2, 4 and 5 from op 19
78rpm issue: eterna 120 024 (no 4 only)
melodiya lp issues: D 015891-015892 and SM 04125-04126
further issues: colosseum CRLP 232 and eurodisc KK 86616

CHS 1312   works by beethoven and mendelssohn

emil gilels, piano

beethoven piano sonata no 2 in c op 2 no 3

recorded in 1952 in moscow

melodiya 78rpm issue: 021621-021626

melodiya lp issues: D 02305-02306 and D 04329-04330

further issue: H 1612

mendelssohn piano concerto no 1 in g minor

recorded on 4 may 1953 in moscow

all-union symphony orchestra

kyrill kondrashin, conductor

melodiya lp issue: D 014775-014776

further issue: h 1612

also issued by eurodisc, westminster, emi, monarch, allegro, bruno,
colosseum, classics club, hall of fame and saga

CHS 1313   shostakovich symphony no 10

recorded on 24 april 1954 in philharmonic hall leningrad

leningrad philharmonic orchestra

evgeny mravinsky, conductor

melodiya issues: D 02243-02244 and D 032508-032509

further issues: 2068, colosseum CRLP 173, mk MK 1523, classics club X 1018,
chant du monde LDX 8113 and saga XID 5228

cd: saga SCD 3366 and SCD 9017

CHS 1314   shostakovich seven preludes and fugues from op 87

this edition first published in january 1956

dimitri shostakovich, piano

CHS 1316   prokofiev piano concerto no 1 & rimsky-korsakov piano concerto

recorded on 17 february 1950 (rimsky-korsakov) and in 1952 (prokofiev) in moscow

moscow youth symphony orchestra

kyrill kondrashin, conductor (prokofiev)

kurt sanderling, conductor (rimsky-korsakov)

sviatoslav richter, piano

melodiya 78rpm issues: 670-673 (prokofiev) and 956-957 (rimsky-korsakov)

melodiya lp issues: 00735-00736 (prokofiev), 09897-09898 (prokofiev),
04289-04290 (prokofiev), 0391-0392 (rimsky-korsakov) and
04683-04684 (rimsky-korsakov)

cd: chant du monde LDC 278 950 and rca/bmg 74321 294602

also published on numerous lp labels including chant du monde, bruno, classics club,
musicart, eurodisc, vedette, colosseum, period, discocorp, miro, everest, monitor,
saga, italian emi and american columbia

CHS 1317   khachaturian gayaneh, first & second suites from the ballet
this edition first published in april 1956
bolshoi theatre orchestra
boris khaikin, conductor
melodiya issues: D 2410-2411 and D 2372-2373

CHS 1318 (2-lp)   smetana the bartered bride/sung in russian
this edition first published in may 1956
bolshoi theatre orchestra and chorus
kyrill kondrashin, conductor
e.shumilova, soprano
a.orfenov, tenor
georg nelepp, tenor
m.soloviev, bass
melodiya issues: D 045-050 and M10 035493-035498
excerpts from the recording also on 143

CHS 1500 lp series   1957
after these few initial releases this became an american re-issue series which
included much material not of concert hall origin

CHS 1500   liszt piano concerti no 1 and no 2
this edition first published in june 1957
zürich radio orchestra
walter goehr, conductor
philippe entremont, piano
further issues: 68 and 2325
*piano concerto no 2 was also published in the usa in 1956 as a pre-recorded binaural
stereophonic tape*

CHS 1501   works for piano and orchestra
this edition first published in june 1957
netherlands philharmonic orchestra
philippe entremont, piano
rachmaninov piano concerto no 2
walter goehr, conductor
further issues: 214, 2062 and 2909 and festival classique FC 424
franck variations symphoniques pour piano et orchestre
carl bamberger, conductor
further issues: 2062, 2909 and festival classique FC 242
*rachmaninov was also published in the usa in 1956 as a pre-recorded binaural stereophonic
tape; franck also re-issued in cd on the american rediscovery label*

CHS 1502   recital of piano music by chopin
this edition first published in june 1957
philippe entremont, piano
further issues: 80, 2792 and in 6-lp set retaining original catalogue number

CHS 1508   see CHS 1068

CHS 1523   rameau platee, first and second suites from the ballet
lausanne chamber orchestra
victor desarzens, conductor
further issue: 86
couperin ballet suite   see CH-H9

H 1600 lp series 1958-1959

this appears to be the final american lp re-issue series, although a concurrent series
with prefix RG (3-digit numbers) is also listed in 1959 schwann catalogues;
the main reason for listing the H series is that it includes the nearest concert
hall came to a systematic issue (on numbers 1656-1661, 1665-1666,
1677-1678 and 1693-1694) of their mozart symphony cycle planned with
conductor otto ackermann but finally completed with henry swoboda
(symphonies 29, 34, 35 and 40), carl bamberger (symphony 32), and walter
goehr (symphonies 33, 36 and 37)

H 1603	see CHS 1303	**H 1612**	see CHS 1312
H 1638	see CH-F4	**H 1639**	see CH-F10
H 1640	see CH-C10 and CHS 1140	**H 1641**	see CH-G11
H 1650	see CHS 1150	**H 1651**	see CHS 1151
H 1653	see CH-E8 and CH-F8	**H 1656**	see CHS 1256
H 1657	see CHS 1257	**H 1658**	see CHS 1258
H 1659	see CHS 1259	**H 1660**	see CHS 1260

H 1661   symphonies by mozart
netherlands philharmonic orchestra
henry swoboda, conductor
symphony no 35 k385 "haffner"
further issue: 75
symphony no 40 k550
further issue: 65
symphony no 40 also issued on cd by american rediscovry label

H 1665	see CHS 1165	**H 1666**	see CHS 1166
H 1677	see CHS 1177	**H 1678**	see CHS 1178
H 1693	see CHS 1193	**H 1694**	see CHS 1194

first release of 10" lps with prefix CM (UK) and MMS (other territories)

1   mozart german dances k605 nos 1 and 5
winterthur symphony orchestra
walter goehr, conductor
symphony no 36 "linz"   see CHS 1259

2   see CHC 23

3   mendelssohn symphony no 4 "italian"
winterthur symphony orchestra
clemens dahinden, conductor

4   chopin piano concerto no 2 in f minor
zürich radio orchestra
walter goehr, conductor
noel mewton-wood, piano
cd: dante HPC 015

5   tchaikovsky 1812 overture; valse melancolique in e minor; marche solennelle in d
musical masterpiece society orchestra
vladimir tergowski, conductor
according to david patmore vladimir tergowski was a pseudonym for walter goehr

6   haydn symphony no 96 "miracle" and overture in g minor
winterthur symphony orchestra
walter goehr, conductor

7   mendelssohn violin concerto in e minor
recorded in hilversum
netherlands philharmonic orchestra
otto ackermann, conductor
louis kaufman, violin
further issues: nixa MLPY 7, classic (france) 11001 and classics club X 71

8   beethoven piano sonata op 57 "appassionata" and mendelssohn lieder ohne worte nos 25 and 35
ella goldstein, piano

9   mozart piano concerto no 20 k466
musical masterpiece society orchestra
walter goehr, conductor
frank pelleg, piano

10   beethoven symphony no 8 in f op 93 and twelve contretänze
winterthur symphony orchestra
walter goehr, conductor
further issues of the contretänze: 973, 2159, 2294, 5219-5220 & 6244
selection from the contretänze also on 2297

11   bizet symphony in c
utrecht symphony orchestra
paul hupperts, conductor

12   tchaikovsky piano concerto no 1 op 23
musical masterpiece society orchestra
walter goehr, conductor
noel mewton-wood, piano
cd: pristine audio PASC 114

13   bach brandenburg concerti nos 4 and 5

winterthur symphony orchestra
walter goehr, conductor
peter rybar, violin
peter lukas graf, flute
frank pelleg, piano

14   lalo symphonie espagnole pour violon et orchestre
utrecht symphony orchestra
walter goehr, conductor
ricardo odnoposoff, violin
further issue: RG 113
cd: doremi DHR 7874-7879

15   brahms haydn variations and academic festival overture
utrecht symphony orchestra
paul hupperts, conductor
further issues: RG 120 (overture) and 2058 (variations)

16   tchaikovsky symphony no 4 in f minor op 36
recorded in hilversum
netherlands philharmonic orchestra
walter goehr, conductor

17   beethoven piano concerto no 2 in b flat op 19
winterthur symphony orchestra
walter goehr, conductor
artur balsam, piano

18   beethoven violin sonata no 9 "kreutzer"

oliver colbentson, violin
david garvey, piano

19   schumann fantasia in c

grant johannesen, piano

20   see CHC 61

21   chopin piano sonata no 2 op 35 and fantaisie-impromptu op 66
robert goldsand, piano

22   beethoven symphony no 5 in c minor op 67
tonhalle-orchester zürich
otto ackermann, conductor
cd: datum DAT 12324

23   see CHS 1256 and CHS 1260

24   beethoven piano concerto no 4 in g op 58
utrecht symphony orchestra
walter goehr, conductor
noel mewton-wood, piano
cd: dante HPC 106, pristine audio PASC 116 and abc classics 461 9002

25   beethoven piano concerto no 3 in c minor op 37
recorded in hilversum
netherlands philharmonic orchestra
walter goehr, conductor
grant johannesen, piano

26   see CHS 1401

27   orchestral music by dukas and mussorgsky
l'apprenti sorcier
utrecht symphony orchestra
paul hupperts, conductor
night on bare mountain
netherlands philharmonic orchestra
walter goehr, conductor

28   brahms symphony no 3 in f op 90
recorded in january 1953 in zürich
tonhalle-orchester zürich
otto ackermann, conductor
further issue: otto-ackermann-archiv OAA 104

29   wagner meistersinger overture & act 3 prelude & tannhäuser overture
recorded in january 1953 in zürich
tonhalle-orchester zürich
otto ackermann, conductor
further issue: otto-ackermann-archiv OAA 104 (tannhäuser)

30   see CHS 1127
31   see CHC 60

32   recital of organ works by bach
alexander schreiner, organ

33   beethoven symphony no 7 in a op 92
tonhalle-orchester zürich
otto ackermann, conductor
cd: datum DAT 12324

34   tchaikovsky violin concerto in d op 35
recorded in 1952 in hilversum
netherlands philharmonic orchestra
walter goehr, conductor
ricardo odnoposoff, violin
further issue: 3056
cd: doremi DHR 7874-7879

35   see CHS 1153

36   dvorak symphony no 9 in e minor "new world"
tonhalle-orchester zürich
otto ackermann, conductor
further issues: 3064 and 6010 in set 6001-6013
cd: datum DAT 12324

37   mozart clarinet quintet k581
quatuor pascal
peter simonauer, clarinet

38   see CHS 1198

39   schubert piano quintet "the trout"
winterthur string quartet
pina pozzi, piano

40   works for violin and orchestra
ricardo odnoposoff, violin
bruch violin concerto in g minor
recorded in 1953 in hilversum
netherlands philharmonic orchestra
walter goehr, conductor
cd: doremi DHR 7874-7879
paganini la campanella
utrecht symphony orchestra
paul hupperts, conductor

41   schumann piano quintet op 44
quatuor pascal
hannes kann, piano

42   see CHS 1141 and CHS 1157

43   schumann piano concerto in a minor
recorded in hilversum
netherlands philharmonic orchestra
walter goehr, conductor
noel mewton-wood, piano
cd: pristine audio PASC 149
also issued on cd in america on the rediscovery label

44   beethoven piano sonatas nos 14 and 23
recorded in 1952
hannes kann, piano
cd: pristine audio PAKM 033

45   beethoven piano concerto no 5 op 73 "emperor"
recorded in hilversum
netherlands philharmonic orchestra
otto ackermann, conductor
hannes kann, piano
further issue: world records T 13

46   mozart piano concerto no 24 in c minor k491
recorded in hilversum
netherlands philharmonic orchestra
otto ackermann, conductor
grant johannesen, piano
further issue: 6001 in set 6001-6013

47   haydn string quartets op 33 no 2 and op 76 no 3
recorded in 1948
quatuor pascal
cd: pristine audio PACM 064

48   see CHS 1214
49   see CHS 1138

50   mozart piano concerto no 25 in c k503
tonhalle-orchester zürich
otto ackermann, conductor
frank pelleg, piano

51   schubert symphony no 8 d759 "unfinished"
tonhalle-orchester zürich
otto ackermann, conductor

52   beethoven piano sonatas nos 8 "pathetique" and 31
grant johannesen, piano

53   chamber music by debussy
cello sonata   see CH-A10
string quartet
quatuor pascal
cd: pristine audio PACM 031

54   violin works by bach
ricardo odnoposoff, violin
violin concerto no 2 in e bwv 1042
recorded in 1952 in hilversum
netherlands philharmonic orchestra
walter goehr, conductor
cd: doremi DHR 7874-7879
chaconne from the solo partita in d minor

55   concerti by haydn
trumpet concerto in e flat
frankfurt chamber orchestra
carl bamberger, conductor
herbert bräunig, trumpet
further issues: 519 and 2101
flute concerto in d
winterthur symphony orchestra
clemens dahinden, conductor
willi urfer, flute
further issues: 211 and 2101

56   see CH-AR

57   orchestral works by rimsky-korsakov   see CHS 1106
mussorgsky khovantschina prelude
winterthur symphony orchestra
victor desarzens, conductor

58   franck symphony in d minor

recorded in hilversum
netherlands philharmonic orchestra
walter goehr, conductor
further issue: 5028

59   haydn symphonies nos 94 "surprise" and 100 "military"
recorded in hilversum
netherlands philharmonic orchestra
henry swoboda, conductor

60   mendelssohn symphony no 3 "scotch"
recorded in hilversum
netherlands philharmonic orchestra
walter goehr, conductor

61   see CHS 1160 and CHS 1316

62   saint-saens violin concerto no 3 and havanaise
recorded in hilversum
netherlands philharmonic orchestra
maurits van den berg, conductor
louis kaufman, violin

63 works by schubert
symphony no 3 in d d200
utrecht symphony orchestra
paul hupperts, conductor
adagio and rondo in f d487 for piano and strings
winterthur symphony orchestra
clemens dahinden, conductor
frank pelleg, piano

64 works by stravinsky
l'oiseau de feu, suite from the ballet
recorded in hilversum
amsterdam philharmonic society
walter goehr, conductor
also issued in 1956 in america as a pre-recorded binaural stereophonic tape
concerto for piano and winds see CHS 1160

65 see CHS 1258 and H 1661

66 orchestral works by tchaikovsky
romeo and juliet, fantasy overture
recorded in hilversum
netherlands philharmonic orchestra
walter goehr, conductor
further issue: 176
voyevode and elegy for strings see CH-G7

67 see CHS 1155 and CHS 1316
68 see CHS 1500

69 russian choral music for christmas and lent

don cossack choir
serge jaroff, conductor

70 see CHC 59

71 christmas carols
pro arte motettenchor
peter mark, conductor
heinz wehrle, organ

72   **recital of harpsichord music by bach**
günther ramin, harpsichord

73   **orchestral music by strauss and liszt**
utrecht symphony orchestra
tod und verklärung
ignace neumark, conductor
les preludes
paul hupperts, conductor
further issue: RG 145 (both works)
both works also issued in 1956 in america as pre-recorded binaural
stereophnic tape; tod und verklärung also issued on cd in america
on the rediscovery label

74   **works by bach**
winterthur symphony orchestra
orchestral suite no 1 bwv1066
henry swoboda, conductor
orchestral suite no 2 bwv1067
clemens dahinden, conductor
peter lukas graf, flute
further issue: RG 130 (suite no 2)

75   see CHS 1257 and H 1661

76   **works by de falla**

el amor brujo
recorded in hilversum
netherlands philharmonic orchestra
walter goehr, conductor
anny delorie, contralto
further issue: 2253
also issued in 1956 in america as a pre-recorded binaural stereophonic tape
canciones populares espanolas
cora canne-meyer, mezzo-soprano
liesbeth ruemke-hoppen, piano

77   **concerti by bach**
winterthur symphony orchestra
clemens dahinden, conductor
concerto in d minor for oboe and violin bwv 1060
egon parolari, oboe
peter rybar, violin
concerto in c for two keyboards
hans andreae and theodor sack, harpsichords

78   beethoven trio in b flat op 97 "archduke"

serge blanc, violin
leo rostal, cello
leo nadelmann, piano

79   brahms piano sonata no 3 in f minor

leo nadelmann, piano

80   see CHS 1502

81   concertante works by debussy
recorded in hilversum
netherlands philharmonic orchestra
walter goehr, conductor
premiere rapsodie pour clarinette et orchestre
jos d'hondt, clarinet
fantaisie pour piano et orchestre   see CH-G9

82   faure requiem
orchestre et choeurs philharmoniques de paris
rene leibowitz, conductor
nadine sautereau, soprano
bernard demigny, baritone

83   schubert string quartet d804

quatuor pascal

84   see CH-E2, CH-G6 and CH-H16

85   handel concerti grossi op 6 nos 6 and 12

winterthur symphony orchestra
clemens dahinden, conductor
peter rybar, violin

86   works by rameau
platee, first and second suites from the ballet music   see CHS 1523
pieces de clavecin, selection
theodor sack, harpsichord

87   concerti by mozart
horn concerto no 4 k495   see CH-H3
flute concerto no 2 k314
winterthur symphony orchestra
henry swoboda, conductor
aurele nicolet, flute

88   prokofiev peter and the wolf
recorded in hilversum
netherlands philharmonic orchestra
otto ackermann, conductor
spoken narration dubbed in various languages
further issue: 2886

89   see CH-A8 and CH-G8

7" lps (33.1/3rpm) with prefix CM (UK) and MMS (other territories)

91   overtures by schubert
recorded in hilversum
rosamunde overture
musical masterpiece society orchestra
walter goehr, conductor
overture in the italian style d591 see CH-F6

92   corelli concerto grosso no 8 in g minor "christmas"
winterthur symphony orchestra
clemens dahinden, conductor

93   bach brandenburg concerto no 3
recorded in hilversum
netherlands philharmonic orchestra
walter goehr, conductor
further issue: 6101 in set 6101-6112

94   mozart serenade no 13 k525 "eine kleine nachtmusik"
recorded in hilversum
netherlands philharmonic orchestra
walter goehr, conductor
further issue: 6101 in set 6101-6112

95   grieg peer gynt, first suite from the incidental music
recorded in hilversum
amsterdam philharmonic society
walter goehr, conductor

96   bizet carmen, orchestral suite from the opera
recorded in hilversum
amsterdam philharmonic society
walter goehr, conductor
issued on cd in america on the rediscovery label

97   beethoven egmont and coriolan overtures
recorded in hilversum
netherlands philharmonic orchestra
walter goehr, conductor
further issue: 937

98   mozart don giovanni and entführung overtures
tonhalle-orchester zürich
otto ackermann, conductor

continuation of 10" lps with prefix CM (UK) and MMS (other territories)

99   see CHS 1166

101   see CHS 1133

102   see CH-G9 and CHS 1181

103   handel the water music
recorded in hilversum
netherlands philharmonic orchestra
carl bamberger, conductor
further issues: RG 144,   2060 and 3058
also issued in 1956 in american as a pre-recorded binaural stereophonic tape

104   see CHS 1064

105   see CH-E8 and CH-F4

106   see CHS 1159

107   instrumental music by stravinsky
duo concertant for violin and piano
louis kaufman, violin
helene pignari, piano
suite italienne pour violoncello et piano
raya garbousova, cello
erich itor-kahn, piano

108   works by milhaud
recorded in hilversum
la cheminee du roi rene and quatuor pour vents
netherlands philharmonic wind quintet
further issue: decca (usa) DL 1956
symphonies   see CH-B11

109   brahms violin sonata op 78
louis kaufman, violin
helene pignari, piano
further issue: classics club X 83

110   bach selection from the anna magdalena orgelbüchlein
piet van egmond, organ

111 (2-lp)   verdi rigoletto
recorded in 1954 in hilversum
netherlands philharmonic orchestra and chorus
walter goehr, conductor
hedda heuser, soprano
anny delorie, contralto
paul conrad, tenor
paolo gorin, baritone
henk driessen, baritone
gee smith, bass
excerpts from the recording also issued on 5016 in set 5010-5022

112 (2-lp)   rossini il barbiere di siviglia
recorded in 1952 in hilversum
netherlands philharmonic orchestra and chorus
alexander krannhals, conductor
cora canne meyer, mezzo-soprano
nel duval, contralto
paul conrad, tenor
paolo gorin, baritone
guus hoekman, baritone
anton eldering, bass
further issue: OP 6
excerpts from the recording also on 920, 3061 and 5013 in set 5010-5022

113 (2-lp) mozart die entführung aus dem serail

recorded on 1 may 1954 in cologne
gürzenich-orchester köln
chor der oper köln
otto ackermann, conductor
marilyn tyler, soprano
helen petrich, soprano
john van kesteren, tenor
karl schiebener, tenor
august griebel, bass
further issues: OP 17 and discophilia 20-21
open reel tape: RX 52
cd: gala GL 100 809
excerpts from the recording also on 5010 in set 5010-5022

114 (2-lp) mussorgsky boris godunov, scenes from the opera

taken from a complete recording made in march 1948 in moscow
bolshoi theatre orchestra and chorus
nikolai golovanov, conductor
maria maksakova and alexandra tourtchina, mezzo-sopranos
georgi nelepp and maxim mikhailov, tenors
mark reizen, bass
further issue: OP 13
*complete recording issued by melodiya, colosseum, dante, arlecchino,
arkadia, aquarius and audio enterprises*

115 (2-lp) bizet les pecheurs de perles

recorded in 1951
orchestre et choeurs symphoniques de paris
rene leibowitz, conductor
mattiwilda dobbs, soprano
enzo seri, tenor
jean borthayre, baritone
lucien mans, bass
further issues: nixa PLP 205, counterpoint 12005, everest S-422 and
renaissance SX 205
cd: preiser 20010

116 (2-lp) verdi un ballo in maschera

recorded in 1951
orchestre et choeurs symphoniques de paris
rene leibowitz, conductor
ethel semser, soprano
marie-therese kahn, mezzo-soprano
joachim karol, tenor
jean borthayre, baritone
further issues: 6334-6335 in 6-lp set of verdi operas, renaissance SX 207,
classic (france) 6182-6184 and period TE 1082
cd: hamburger archiv für gesangskunst 30075

117 (2-lp) weber oberon
recorded in 1953 in stuttgart
orchester und chor des süddeutschen rundfunks
hans müller-kray, conductor
helene bader, paula bauer and friederike sailer, sopranos
karl liebl and franz fehringer, tenors
robert titze, baritone
further issues: period SPL 575 and TE 1012 and counterpoint MC 20057

118 (2-lp) offenbach la belle helene
recorded in 1952
orchestre et choeurs philharmoniques de paris
rene leibowitz, conductor
janine linda, soprano
andre dran, tenor
roger giraud, baritone
further issues: 2036, classic (france) 6140-6141, musidisc FC 253,
renaissance SX 206, nixa PLP 206, everest S-458 and vogue MCM 120 006

119 schubert piano trio no 1 d471
leo nadelmann, piano
serge blanc, violin
leo rostal, cello

120 beethoven symphony no 6 in f op 68 "pastoral"
recorded in hilvrsum
netherlands philharmonic orchestra
walter goehr, conductor
further issue: 2001

121   see CH-G2
122   see CHS 1130

123   works by grieg and smetana
walter goehr, conductor
piano concerto
recorded in hilversum
netherlands philharmonic orchestra
grant johannesen, piano
further issue: 2002
also re-issued on cd in america on the rediscovery label
dance and furiant from the bartered bride
orchester der oper frankfurt
further issue: 5219-5220

124   dvorak cello concerto in b minor

tonhalle-orchester zürich
otto ackermann, conductor
paul tortelier, cello
further issue: 2006
cd: datum DAT 12324

125   mendelssohn a midsummer night's dream, incidental music
recorded in hilversum
netherlands philharmonic orchestra
walter goehr, conductor
further issue: 2005

126   rimsky-korsakov scheherazade, symphonic suite
recorded in hilversum
netherlands philharmonic orchestra
walter goehr, conductor
further issue: 2004
also re-issued on cd in america on the rediscovery label

127   gounod faust, scenes from the opera
recorded in hilversum
netherlands philharmonic orchestra and chorus
walter goehr, conductor
uta graf, soprano
anneke van den greef, mezzo-soprano
leo larsen, tenor
jan kruls, baritone
paolo gorin, bass
further issues: 2020 and OP 11

128   see CHS 1152

129   symphonies by haydn
no 46 in b   see CH-G14
no 96 in d "miracle"
winterthur symphony orchestra
walter goehr, conductor

130   johann strauss der zigeunerbaron, scenes from the operetta
zürich radio orchestra and chorus
walter goehr, conductor
uta graf, hedda heuser and rita pich, sopranos
albert kunz, tenor
mathias schmid and karel pistorius, baritones
further issues: 2025, 2884 in set 2880-2885 and OP 12
excerpts from the recording also on 910

131   see CHS 1125
132   see CHS 1140
133   see CHS 1230

134D   lehar das land des lächelns, scenes from the operetta
sinfonieorchester des hessischen rundfunks
carl bamberger, conductor
edith berg and hilde breyer, sopranos
kurt wolinski, tenor

134F   lehar das land des lächelns, scenes from the operetta in french
orchestre lamoureux
francois le berger, conductor
uta graf and hilde breyer, sopranos
aime doniat, tenor

135D   lehar die lustige witwe, scenes from the operetta
opera society orchestra
georg walter, conductor
hilde breyer, soprano
kurt herbert, tenor
also issued in 1956 in america as a pre-recorded binaural steeophonic tape

135F   lehar die lustige witwe, scenes from the operetta in french
orchestre philharmonique de paris
francois le berger, conductor
uta graf, soprano
aime doniat, tenor

136   kalman gräfin maritza, scenes from the operetta
opera society orchestra
carl bamberger, conductor
hilde breyer, soprano
kurt herbert, tenor

137   see CHS 1169

138   works by mussorgsky and borodin
mussorgsky-ravel pictures from an exhibition
recorded in hilversum
netherlands philharmonic orchestra
walter goehr, conductor
in the steppes of central asia
utrecht symphony orchestra
paul hupperts, conductor
further issue: 2064 (both works)
editions of this record appear to have been published both with and without the borodin as fill-up;
mussorgsky pictures also issued in 1956 in america as a pre-recorded binaural stereophonic tape

139   see CHC 48

140   offenbach orfee aux enfers, scenes from the operetta
recorded in 1952 and taken from a complete recording
orchestre et choeurs philharmoniques de paris
rene leibowitz, conductor
claudine collart, soprano
ann-marie carpenter, mezzo-soprano
bernard demigny and jean mollien, tenors
complete recording published by musidisc, classic (france), renaissance, nixa, vogue, preiser,
regis and andromeda

141 (2-lp) puccini la boheme
opera society orchestra and chorus
carl bamberger, conductor
marilyn tyler, soprano
corrie bijster, mezzo-soprano
david garen, tenor
igor gorin, baritone
leonardo wolovsky, bass
further issue: 6314-6315 in 6-lp set of puccini operas
open-reel tape: TBN 9
also issued in 1956 in america as a pre-recorded binaural stereophonic tape; excerpts
from the recording also on 2927 and 5021 in set 5010-5022

142 (2-lp) gluck orfee et euridice
recorded in hilversum
netherlands philharmonic orchestra and chorus
nicholas goldschmidt, conductor
annette de la bije, soprano
corrie bijster, mezzo-soprano
leon combe, tenor
excerpts from the recording also on 5010 in set 5010-5022

143   see CHS 1318

144   bach goldberg variations
günther ramin, harpsichord

145   brahms violin concerto in d op 77
recorded in 1954
orchester der oper frankfurt
carl bamberger, conductor
ricardo odnoposoff, violin
further issues: 6105 in set 6101-6112 and crewell collier record guild 121
cd: doremi DHR 7874-7879
also issued in 1956 in america as a pre-recorded binaural stereophonic tape

146   orchestral works by ravel
bolero
recorded in hilversum
netherlands philharmonic orchestra
walter goehr, conductor
further issues: 203 and 2938
also issued in 1956 in america as a pre-recorded binaural stereophonic tape
ma mere l'oye
orchestre pasdeloup
louis martin, conductor
further issue: RG 129, 591, 2583, 2928 and 5201-5202

147   brahms symphony no 2 in d op 73
orchester der oper frankfurt
carl bamberger, conductor
further issue: 2058

148   orchestral works by schumann and mendelssohn
symphony no 1 in b flat "spring"
recorded in hilversum
netherlands philharmonic orchestra
carl bamberger, conductor
die schöne melusine overture   see CH-E 13

149   works by gershwin
concert hall orchestra
rhapsody in blue
walter goehr, conductor
philippe entremont, piano
further issues: RG 123, 202, 2814, 7024 and festival classique FC 412
also issued in 1956 in america as a pre-recorded binaural stereophnic tape
an american in paris
john walther, conductor
further issue: RG 123

150   french christmas carols
chorale jannequin
jean perisson, conductor

151   see CHS 1161

152   beethoven piano concerto no 1 in c op 15
orchester der oper frankfurt
carl bamberger, conductor
robert goldsand, piano

153   tchaikovsky casse noisette, suite from the ballet

orchester der oper frankfurt
walter goehr, conductor
further issues: 500, 6009 in set 6001-5013 and 6109 in set 6101-6113
also issued in 1956 in america as a pre-recorded binaural stereophonic tapee
saint-saens le carnaval des animaux   see CHS 1179

154   see CHC 45

155   beethoven piano concerto no 2 in b flat op 19
orchester der oper frankfurt
carl bamberger, conductor
robert goldsand, piano

156   lieder by beethoven: an die ferne geliebte; adelaide; gellert-lieder
inez matthews, mezzo-soprano
ralph herbert, baritone
benjamin oren and lowell farr, pianos

157   bach keyboard concerti in d minor and f minor
winterthur symphony orchestra
clemens dahinden, conductor
grant johannesen, piano

158   see CHS 1132

159   **concerti grossi by corelli**
boyd neel chamber orchestra
walter goehr, conductor

160   **french chansons of the sixteenth century**
chorale jannequin
jean perisson, conductor

161   **gershwin piano concerto in f and variations on "i got rhythm"**
concert hall orchestra
walter goehr, conductor
sondra bianca, piano
further issues: RG 123 (concerto), 202 (variations) and festival
classique FC 412

162   **brahms variations and fugue on a theme by handel**

philippe entremont, piano

163   see CH-C6
165   see CHS 1128

166   **liszt les preludes & hungarian fantasy for piano and orchestra**
sinfonieorchester des norddeutschen rundfunks
carl bamberger, conductor
sondra bianca, piano
further issues: 976 (fantasy), 3065 and 6007 in set 6001-6013 (fantasy)

167   **johann strauss eine nacht in venedig, scenes from the operetta**
frankfurter operettenorchester
arthur schmittenbecher, conductor
hilde breyer, soprano
willy müller, tenor

168   **strauss don juan and till eulenspiegels lustige streiche**
sinfonieorchester des hessischen rundfunks
otto ackermann, conductor
further issue: 2808

175   see CHS 1132 and CHS 1133

176   **orchestral works by tchaikovsky**
capriccio italien
recorded between 23-27 february 1959 in the wembley town hall
london philharmonic orchestra
sir adrian boult, conductor
further issues: 939, 3045, 3057, 6013 in set 6001-6013 and
perfect (usa) 13001/15001
romeo and juliet, fantasy overture   see CM 66

177   **tchaikovsky piano concerto no 1 op 23**
orchestre des concerts de paris
carl bamberger, conductor
sondra bianca, piano
further issues: 3050, 6007 in set 6001-6013 and 6109 in set 6101-6113
also re-issued on cd in america on the rediscovery label

178   **enescu rumanian rhapsody no 1 and rimsky-korsakov**
russian easter festival overture
recorded in hilversum
amsterdam philharmonic society
pierre dervaux, conductor
further issue: 5211-5212 (enescu)

179   **schubert symphony no 8 d759 "unfinished"**
orchestre pasdeloup
carl bamberger, conductor
further issues: 5003, 6004 in set 6001-6013 and 6104 in set 6101-6113

181   **mozart piano sonata in c minor k457 & fantasy in c minor k475**
lili kraus, piano

182   **weber-berlioz aufforderung zum tanz**
orchestre des concerts de paris
pierre dervaux, conductor
further issues: 960, 984, 5213-5214 and 6275 in set 6270-6279
chabrier marche joyeuse and fete polonaise; adam si j'etais roi overture
orchestre des concerts de paris
pierre-michel le conte, conductor

185   see CHS 1157
186   see CHS 1126

188   beethoven symphony no 1 in c op 21
orchester der oper frankfurt
walter goehr, conductor
further issues: 2034 and 2201

190   christmas music from the eighteenth century
torelli christmas concerto
netherlands philharmonic orchestra
maurits van den berg, conductor
corelli concerto grosso no 8 in c minor
concert hall orchestra
david josefowitz, conductor
further issues: 963 and 2380
bach sinfonia from the weihnachtsoratorium   see 2057

192   tchaikovsky sleeping beauty, selection from the ballet
rome opera orchestra
walter goehr, conductor
orchestre des concerts de paris
gianfranco rivoli, conductor
further issue: 996 (items conducted by goehr)

196   addinsell warsaw concerto; alfven swedish rhapsody no 1;
bath cornish rhapsody
concert hall orchestra
fred hendrik, conductor
george vincent, piano
further issues: 202 (warsaw concerto) and 7024 (warsaw concerto)

197   beethoven symphony no 8 in f op 93
sinfonieorchester des hessischen rundfunks
walter goehr, conductor
further issue: 2172

198   concerti by weber
konzertstück for piano and orchestra
orchester der wiener staatsoper
victor desarzens, conductor
lili kraus, piano
further issues: 2327, festival classique FC 428 and vanguard SRV 293
cd: scribendum SC 018
clarinet concerto in f minor
netherlands philharmonic orchestra
otto ackermann, conductor
jos d'hondt, clarinet
further issue: 5216-5217

199   lehar der zarewitsch, scenes from the operetta
wiener operettenorchester und –chor
boris mersson, conductor
gerry gross and hea reuss, sopranos
fred bongers, tenor
franz müller, baritone

200   see CHS 1194 and CHS 1257

201   spohr duo in d for two violins; haydn andante and presto
recorded in march 1961 in paris
david oistrakh, violin
igor oistrakh, violin and viola
melodiya issues: D 14121-14122 and S 0579-0580
further issues: 2291 (spohr), monitor MC 2058 and chant du monde LDX 8280
cd: chant du monde LDC 278906, doremi DHR 7714 and notablu 93.5107

202   see 149, 161 and 196

203   orchestral works by ravel
la valse
orchestre des concerts colonne
pierre dervaux, conductor
further issues: 217, 2174 and 2583
bolero   see 146

204   lehar der graf von luxemburg, scenes sung in french
orchestre et choeurs des concerts de paris
boris mersson, conductor
andrea guiot, soprano
remy corazza, tenor

205   see CH-H4

206   recital of guitar music
suzanne bloch, guitar

207   schumann symphony no 2 in c op 61/mercury recording
recorded on 2 december 1955 in old orchestra hall detroit
detroit symphony orchestra
paul paray, conductor
mercury issues: MG 50102/SR 90102/MRL 2519/MMA 11065/
MGW 14061/SRW 18061
cd: philips mercury 462 9552

208 schubert symphony no 8 d759 "unfinished"
recorded on 3 june 1964 in the konzerthaus vienna
wiener symphoniker
josef krips, conductor
further issues: 503, 2341, 2942, 3062, 5005 in set 5004-5009
and 6204 in set 6201-6212
cd: ages 509.0062
orchestra described on this recording as vienna festival orchestra

209 chopin-douglas les sylphides, suite from the ballet
orchestre des concerts de paris
boris mersson, conductor
further issue: 2288 and 6436 in set 6436-6441
excerpts from the recording also on 5203-5204

211 concerti by haydn
keyboard concerto in d
radio geneva orchestra
pierre colombo, conductor
isabelle nef, harpsichord
further issues: 2230, 3074 and 5205-5206
trumpet concerto in e flat see 55

214 see CHS 1501

216 delibes coppelia and sylvia, suites from the ballets
orchestre des concerts de paris
walter goehr, conductor
further issues: 5023-5024, 6437 in set 6436-6441 (coppelia) and

6438 in set 6436-6441 (sylvia)

217 orchestral works by ravel
rapsodie espagnol
orchestre des concerts colonne
pierre dervaux, conductor
further issue: 2174
la valse see 203

218 mendelssohn symphony no 4 "italian"
recorded in april 1961 in bern during a visit to switzerland
halle orchestra
sir john barbirolli, conductor
further issues: 2248, 5006-5007, 5032 and 5034-5035

219   beethoven symphony no 1 in c op 21
orchester des südwestfunks baden-baden
paul kletzki, conductor
further issues: 2201, 2313 and 2695

**221   tchaikovsky 1812 overture and waltz from evgeny
onegin; glinka russlan and lyudmila overture;
mussorgsky gopak from sorotchinsky fair**
recorded in hilversum
amsterdam philharmonic society
pierre dervaux, conductor
further issues: 2173 (all works), 2198 (all works), 3047 (onegin),
5213-5214 and 5219-5220
2198 contained borodin steppes of central asia instead of mussorgsky gopak

**225   favourite overtures
weber oberon; mendelssohn ruy blas;   nicolai die lustigen weiber**
recorded in september 1962 in baden-baden
sinfonieorchester des südwestfunks baden-baden
carl schuricht, conductor
further issues: 2293, 5225-5226 (oberon and lustigen weiber), in
commemorative multiple-lp set carl achuricht and
columbia (japan) OW 7884
cd: scribendum SC 011
suppe dichter und bauer
orchester der wiener staatsoper
walter goehr, conductor
further issue: 2211

227   beethoven symphony no 8 in f op 93/philips recording
recorded in june 1959 in the concertgebouw amsterdam
residentieorkest den haag
willem van otterloo, conductor
philips fontana issues: 698 031CL and 200 006WGL
further lp issue: epic (usa) BC 1059
cd: challenge classics CC 72142

228   schumann cello concerto
orchester der wiener staatsoper
pierre-michel le conte, conductor
aldo parisot, cello
further issues: 2190 and 3076

229   see CHS 1257

301   **oscar straus ein walzertraum, scenes from the operetta**
wiener operettenensemble
oscar straus, conductor
marta rohs and ruthilde boesch, sopranos
rudolf christ, tenor
georg oeggl and karl wagner, baritones

**500 and 900 series: 7" discs playing at 33.1/3rpm and containing
material re-issued from the main concert hall catalogue**
details included under each work's original issue number

**main 2000 series of 12" lps with prefixes AM/BM/CM/SMSA/SMSB/
SMSC (uk) and prefixes MMS/SMS (other european territories)
1961 onwards**
SMSA/SMSB/SMSC denoted recordings published in synchro-stereo format

**2001   orchestral works by beethoven
die geschöpfe des prometheus overture**
recorded in hilversum
netherlands philharmonic orchestra
walter goehr, conductor
symphony no 6 "pastoral"   see 120

**2002   works by grieg
holberg suite**
recorded in hilversum
netherlands philharmonic orchestra
maurits van den berg, conductor
piano concerto see 123

2003   concerti by mozart
musical masterpiece society orchestra
walter goehr, conductor
violin concerto no 5 k219
theo olof, violin
clarinet concerto k622
jos d'hondt, clarinet

2004   see 126

2005   works by mendelssohn

midsummer night's dream overture & incidental music see 125
hebrides overture
tonhalle-orchester zürich
walter goehr, conductor

2006   see 124
2007   see CHS 1113

2008   verdi il trovatore, scenes from the opera
recorded in hilversum
netherlands philharmonic orchestra and chorus
walter goehr, conductor
margit opawski, soprano
anny delorie, contralto
leo larsen, tenor
garfield swift, baritone
siemen jongsma, bass
excerpts from the recording also on 5016 in set 5010-5022

2009   bizet carmen, scenes from the opera
recorded in hilversum
netherlands philharmonic orchestra and chorus
walter goehr, conductor
corey van beckum, soprano
cora canne-meyer, mezzo-soprano
leo larsen, tenor
gerard holthaus, baritone

2010   mozart le nozze di figaro, scenes from the opera
recorded in 1953 in hilversum
netherlands philharmonic orchestra
walter goehr, conductor
margit opawski and anneke van den graf, sopranos
cora canne-meyer, mezzo-soprano
siemen jongsma and henk driessen, baritones
excerpts from the recording also on 5010 in set 5010-5022

2011   **verdi la traviata, scenes from the opera**
recorded in 1953 in hilversum
netherlands philharmonic orchestra
walter goehr, conductor
margit opawski, soprano
leo larsen, tenor
jan vroons and henk driessen, baritones

2012   see CHS 1305

2013 (3-lp) mozart don giovanni/nixa recording
recorded in 1950 in the konzerthaus vienna
wiener symphoniker
chor der wiener staatsoper
hans swarowsky, conductor
hilde konetzni, gertrud grob-prandl and hedda heusser, sopranos
herbert handt, tenor
alfred poell, baritone
mariano stabile and alois pernerstorfer, basses
nixa issue: HLP 2030
further issues: 6324-6326 in 7-lp set of mozart operas, haydn
society 2030 and erato ERH 160230
cd: preiser 90166

2014   **tchaikovsky symphony no 6 "pathetique"**
tonhalle-orchester zürich
otto ackermann, conductor
further issue: 6008 in set 6001-6013
also re-issued on cd in america on the rediscovery label

2015 (2-lp) haydn die schöpfung
recorded on 28 march 1943 by reichsrundfunk in the musikverein vienna
wiener philharmoniker
chor der wiener staatsoper
clemens krauss, conductor
trude eipperle and friedl riegler, sopranos
julius patzak, tenor
georg hann and alois pernerstorfer, basses
further issues: nixa HLP 2005, haydn society HSLP 2005, saga
XID 6213-6214, erato LDE 3005-3006/ERM 160062 and
victor (japan) ZL 30927
cd: preiser 90104

2016	see HDL 13	**2017**	see CHS 1303
2018	see CHS 1195	**2019**	see CHS 1245
2020	see 127	**2021**	see CHS 1234

2022   **johann strauss die fledermaus, scenes from the operetta**
zürich radio orchestra and chorus
walter goehr, conductor
uta graf, hedda heusser and rita pich, sopranos
nata tuescher, mezzo-soprano
albert kunz and johannes bartsch, tenors
mathias schmid and richard miller, baritones
further issue: 2882 in 6-lp set of johann strauss recordings
excerpts from the recording also on 910, 5020 in set 5010-5022, 7025 and 7120

2023   see CHS 1237
2024   see CHS 1135
2025   see 130

2026   **mozart mass in c minor k427**/nixa recording
wiener symphoniker
wiener akademiechor
meinhard von zallinger, conductor
rosl schwaiger, soprano
herta töpper, contralto
hugo meyer-welfing, tenor
george london, baritone
nixa issue: HLP 2006
further issues: haydn society HSLP 2006 and erato LDE 3010/ERH 16001

2027 (2-lp)   richard strauss salome

recorded on 20 may 1948 in the dresden studio of mitteldeutscher rundfunk

sächsische staatskapelle dresden
joseph keilberth, conductor
christel goltz, soprano
inger karen, mezzo-soprano
ruth lange, contralto
bernd aldenhoff and rudolf dittrich, tenors
josef herrmann, baritone
other issues: eterna 822 868-869, olympic 9101 and oceanic 302
cd: berlin classics BC 20622
excerpt from the recording also issued by hänssler classics

2028   see CHS 1184

2029 (2-lp) wagner lohengrin, scenes from the opera
orchester und chor der oper frankfurt
carl bamberger, conductor
uta graf, soprano
anneliese schlosshauer, mezzo-soprano
karl liebl, tenor
roland kunz, baritone
leonardo wolovsky, bass
other issue: 6310-6311 in 6-lp set of scenes from wagner operas
excerpts from the recording also on 5014 in set 5010-5022

2030 (2-lp) haydn orfeo ed euridice/haydn society recording
orchester und chor der wiener staatsoper
hans swarowsky, conductor
judith hellwig and hedda heusser, sopranos
herbert handt, tenor
alfred poell, baritone
haydn society issue: HSLP 2029
other issue: vox OPBX 193

2031   beethoven symphony no 3 op 55 "eroica"
utrecht symphony orchestra
ignace neumark, conductor

2032   see HDL 18

2033 (2-lp) mozart die zauberflöte, scenes from the opera
recorded in 1955 in hilversum
netherlands philharmonic orchestra and chorus
alexander krannhals, conductor
corry bijster, nel duval and marilyn tyler, sopranos
david garen and chris taverne, tenors
august geschwend, baritone
guus hoekman, bass
other issue: OP 21
excerpts from the recording also on 934, 3063 and 5011 in set 5010-5022

2034 (2-lp) symphonies by beethoven
symphony no 1 in c op 21 see 188
symphony no 9 in d minor op 125 "choral"
recorded in hilversum
netherlands philharmonic orchestra and chorus
walter goehr, conductor
corry bijster, soprano
elisabeth pritchard, contralto
david garen, tenor
leonardo wolovsky, bass
*ninth symphony also issued in 1956 in america as a pre-recorded
binaural stereophonic tape*

2035   see CHS 1247

2036   see 118
2037   see CHS 1255

2038 (2-lp) choral works by verdi
messa da requiem
recorded in hilversum
netherlands philharmonic orchestra and chorus
walter goehr, conductor
corry bijster, soprano
elisabeth pritchard, contralto
david garen, tenor
leonardo wolovsky, bass
te deum and stabat mater/4 pezzi sacri   see CHS 1136

2039 (2-lp) wagner die meistersinger von nürnberg, scenes
recorded in 1956
orchester und chor der oper frankfurt
carl bamberger, conductor
uta graf, soprano
anneliese schlosshauer, mezzo-soprano
karl liebl and jakob rees, tenors
georg stern and gerhard misske, baritones
rudolf gonszar, bass
further issues: 6306-6307 in set 6306-6311, OP 20 and urania USD 1027
open-reel tape: RX 62
cd: gala GL 100 802
excerpts from the recording also on 2679, 5016 in set 5010-5022 and 6111

2040   symphonies by beethoven
orchester der oper frankfurt
symphony no 2 in d op 36
carl bamberger, conductor
symphony no 4 in b flat op 60
walter goehr, conductor

2041   see CHS 1201 and CHS 1202
2042   see CHS 1202 and CHS 1203
2043   see CHS 1203 and CHS 1204
2044   see CHS 1205
2045   see CHS 1206 and CHS 1207
2046   see CHS 1204 and CHS 1208
2047   see CHS 1209 and CHS 1212
2048   see CHS 1210 and CHS 1212
2049   see CHS 1211
2050   see CHS 1213

2051   **song cycles by schumann**
benjamin oren, piano
dichterliebe
ralph herbert, baritone
frauenliebe und –leben
helene vanni, soprano

2052   **lehar lustige witwe & land des lächlens, scenes in english**
opera society orchestra
walter goehr and carl bamberger, conductors
uta graf and mija novich, sopranos
kurt herbert and leslie chabay, tenors

2053   **schumann carnaval and faschingsschwank aus wien**
robert goldsand, piano

2054   see CHS 1215

2055   **schubert mass in a flat d678**
sinfonieorchester des norddeutschen rundfunks
altonaer singakademie
carl bamberger, conductor
anne bollinger and ursula zollenkopf, sopranos
helmut kretschmar, tenor
james pease, baritone

2057 (3-lp)   bach weihnachtsoratorium bwv248
hamburger kammerorchester
thomanerchor leipzig
günther ramin, conductor
helga gabriel, soprano
ursula boese, contralto
leo larsen, tenor
jakob stämpfli, bass
excerpts from this recording also on 190 and 3054

2058   see 15 and 147

2059   **works by mendelssohn for piano and orchestra**
serenade and allegro giocoso
winterthur symphony orchestra
walter goehr, conductor
frank pelleg, piano
piano concerto no 1   see CHS 1127

2060   see 103
2061   see CHS 1259 and CHS 1260
2062   see CHS 1501

2063 (2-lp)   concerti by vivaldi

seven concerti from op 8 nos 5-12   se CHS 1064

concerti in d minor and a for viola d'amore and strings
concert hall chamber orchestra
fred hausdörfer, conductor
jan van helden, viola d'amore

2064   works by mussorgsky and borodin
polovtsian dances/prince igor
utrecht symphony orchestra
paul hupperts, conductor
further issue: 927
pictures from an exhibition and in the steppes of central asia
see 138

2065   brahms piano concerto no 2 in b flat op 83
orchester der oper frankfurt
carl bamberger, conductor
robert goldsand, piano

2066   sonatas by nineteenth century composers
franck violin sonata
louis kaufman, violin
helene pignari, piano
further issues: MMS 103 and classics club X 83
saint-saens clarinet sonata
herbert tichman, clarinet
ruth budnevich, piano

2067   salzburg serenades by mozart
walter goehr, conductor
three divertimenti k136, k137 and k138
boyd neel chamber orchestra
serenata notturna k239
hamburger kammerorchester

2068   see CHS 1313

2069   schubert winterreise
leslie chabay, tenor
benjamin oren, piano

2070   see CHS 1125 and CHS 1126
2071   see 2073 and 2074

2072   vivaldi juditha triumphans,   scenes from the oratorio
orchestra di scuola venezia
coro del teatro fenice
angelo ephrikian, conductor
further issues: 2950 and period SPLP 557
complete work also published on period SPL 533

2074   rossini la cambiale di matrimonio
recorded in 1953 in rome
orchestra and chorus of societa dell quartetto di roma
giuseppe morelli, conductor
angelica tuccari and grazia ciferi, sopranos
giuseppe gentile, tenor
nestore catalani and tito dolciotti, basses
further issues: nixa PLP 583, period SPL 583
and contrepoint (france) MC 20039
excerpts from the recording also on 2071

2075   rossini la scala di seta
recorded in 1953 in rome
orchestra and chorus of societa dell quartetto di roma
giuseppe morelli, conductor
angelica tuccari, soprano
giuseppina salvi, mezzo-soprano
giuseppe gentile and piero besma, tenors
nestore catalani, baritone
tito dolciotti, bass
further issues: nixa PLP 591, period SPL 591
and contrepoint (france) 20063
excerpts from the recording also on 2071

**2076   chamber music by ravel
introduction and allegro**
french radio ensemble
marie-claire jamet, harp
further issue: 2583
string quartet see CHS 1123
violin sonata see CH-E 6

2078 (2-lp) haydn die jahreszeiten

sinfonieorchester und chor des norddeutschen rundfunks
walter goehr, conductor
teresa stich-randall, soprano
helmut kretschmar, tenor
erich wenk, bass
further issues: 6380-6381 in set 6376-6381 and nonesuch HB 73009
xcerpts from the recording also on 5209-5210

2079 bach concerti bwv 1043 and bwv 1044

hamburger kammerorchester
walter goehr, conductor
saschko gavriloff and frederick wührer, violins
gerhard otto, flute
irmgard lechner, harpsichord
further issue: 2846

2080   see CH-H 16 and CHS 1170
2081   see CHS 1070
2082   see CHS 1146
2083   see CHS 1148

2084 instrumental works by schubert
duo for violin and piano d934

louis kaufman, violin
pina pozzi, piano
arpeggione sonata
george rieci, cello
leopold mittmann, piano

2085 (2-lp) beethoven missa solemnis op 123

sinfonieorchester und chor des norddeutschen rundfunks
walter goehr, conductor
uta graf, soprano
grace hoffman, contralto
helmut kretschmar, tenor
erich wenk, bass
further issue: vanguard SRV 214-215
die ruinen von athen overture   see CHS 1158

2086 (2-lp) beethoven the five cello sonatas

janos starker, cello
abba bogin, piano
further issues: period SPL 560-561/SPL 562

2087   brahms the two cello sonatas
janos starker, cello
abba bogin, piano
further issues: period SPL 593, nixa PLP 593 and
contrepoint (france) MC 20070

2088   haydn symphonies nos 101 "clock" and 104 "london"
orchestre pasdeloup
louis martin, conductor
further issues: 2161 (no 101), 2910 (no 101) and in a 6-lp set (no 101)
*symphony 101 also issued in 1956 in america as a pre-recorded binaural
stereophonic tape*

2089   bach die kunst der fuge
hamburger kammerorchester
walter goehr, conductor

2091   orchestral works by brahms
carl bamberger, conductor
symphony no 4 in e minor op 98
orchester der oper frankfurt
further issues: RG 137, 5005 and 6004 in set 6001-6013
tragic overture op 81
sinfonieorchester des norddeutschen rundfunks

2092   mozart violin concerti nos 3 k216 and 4k218
hamburger kammerorchester
walter goehr, conductor
manoug parikian, violin

**2093   wagner tannhäuser bacchanale; parsifal karfreitagszauber;
tristan vorspiel und liebestod; siegfried waldweben**
orchester der oper frankfurt
carl bamberger, conductor
further issue: columbia (usa) HL 7172

2094   berlioz suites from la damnation de faust & romeo et juliette
sinfonieorchester des hessischen rundfunks
pierre-michel le conte, conductor
further issues: 984 (marche hongroise) and 5217-5218

**2095   overtures by rossini and weber: guilleaume tell; la gazza
ladra; der freischütz; abu hassan; oberon**
sinfonieorchester des hessischen rundfunks
pierre-michel le conte, conductor

2096   brahms symphony no 1 in c minor op 68
orchester der oper frankfurt
carl bamberger, conductor
further issue: 6014 in set 6001-6013

2097-2098 (2-lp) bach the six brandenburg concerti
recorded in july 1956 for the american unicorn label
boyd neel orchestra
boyd neel, conductor
unicorn issue: UNLP 1040-1041
further issues: 940 (no 3), 6001 in set 6001-6013 (no 2) and
realistic (usa) 50-0439
these are not to be confused with boyd neel's earlier recordings of the concerti for decca;
*   according to john holmes (conductors on record) this later set featured among its soloists*
*   dennis brain and norman del mar (horns), leon goossens (oboe), emanuel hurwitz*
*   (violin) and george malcolm (harpsichord)*

2099 (2-lp) choral works by brahms
ein deutsches requiem
sinfonieorchester des norddeutschen rundfunks
hamburger singakademie
carl bamberger, conductor
teresa stich-randall, soprano
james pease, baritone
further issues: 2860-2861, in a 6-lp set of choral music and nonesuch HB 73003
cd: agostini SACCD 005
alto rhapsody
sinfonieorchester und chor des norddeutschen rundfunks
carl bamberger, conductor
grace hoffman, contralto
further issues: RG 137 and nonesuch HB 73003
fest und –gedenksprüche
jugendchor der hamburger michaelskirche
f.brinkmann, conductor
further issue: nonesuch HB 73003

2100   violin concerti by dvorak and glazunov
recorded in 1953 in paris
orchestre des concerts de paris
walter goehr, conductor
ricardo odnoposoff, violin
cd: doremi DHR 7874-7879

2101   concerti by haydn
sinfonia concertante in b flat
hamburger kammerorchester
hans-jürgen walther, conductor
frederick wührer, violin
fritz sommer, cello
heinz nordbruch, oboe
fritz henker, basson
trumpet concerto in e flat and flute concerto in d   see 55

2102   lortzing zar und zimmermann, scenes from the singspiel
sinfonieorchester und chor des hessischen rundfunks
georg walter, conductor
hilde breyer, soprano
kurt wolinski, tenor
wilhelm strienz, bass
excerpts from the rcording on 5012 in set 5010-5022

2103   symphonies by mozart
symphony no 35 in d k385 "haffner"
recorded in february 1959 in the town hall wembley
london philharmonic orchestra
sir adrian boult, conductor
further issues: 3055, 5028 and perfect (usa) 13003/15003
symphony no 41 in c k551 "jupiter"
sinfonieorchester des hessischen rundfunks
alexander krannhals, conductor

2104   choral and orchestral works by mozart
sinfonieorchester und chor des norddeutschen rundfunks
walter goehr, conductor
mass in c minor k317 "coronation"
agnes giebel, soprano
ursula zollenkopf, contralto
julius patzak, tenor
heinz rehfuss, baritone
ave verum corpus k618
maurerische trauermusik k477
above works also issued in a 6-lp set of mozart choral music
exsultate jubilate k65
badische staatskapelle
mattiwilda dobbs, soprano
lp also published with number 2104A with same works except maurerische trauermusik

2105   mozart requiem in d minor k626
sinfonieorchester und chor des norddeutschen rundfunks
walter goehr, conductor
dorothea förstl-georgi, soprano
ursula zollenkopf, contralto
julius patzak, tenor
heinz rehfuss, baritone

2106   mozart serenade no 7 in d k250 "haffner"
hamburger kammerorchester
julius patzak, conductor
saschko gavriloff, violin

2107 (2-lp) offenbach les contes d'hoffmann, sung in german

sinfonieorchester und chor des hessischen rundfunks
pierre-michel le conte, conductor
mattiwilda dobbs, lotte laufer and uta graf, sopranos
nata tuescher, mezzo-soprano
david garen, tenor
heinz rehfuss, baritone

2108   (2-lp) offenbach les contes d'hoffmann
recorded in 1958 in paris
orchestre et choeurs des concerts de paris
pierre-michel le conte, conductor
mattiwilda dobbs and uta graf, sopranos
nata tuescher, mezzo-soprano
leopold simoneau and aime doniat, tenors
heinz rehfuss and bernard lefort, baritones
further issues: 6320-6321 in set 6318-6323, epic (usa) SC 6028
and BSC 101 and festival CFC 60016
cd: urania 22349
excerpts from the recording also issued on 5019 in set 5010-5022

2109 (2-lp) smetana the bartered bride, sung in german
recorded in 1954
orchester und chor der oper frankfurt
walter goehr, conductor
elfriede trötschel, soprano
elfriede schlosshauer, mezzo-soprano
kurt wolinski and bruno müller, tenors
heinz rehfuss and karl kümmel, baritones
cd: gala GL 100 810
excerpts from the recording also issued on 3052 and on 5018 in set 5010-5022

2111   mozart string quartets no 1 k155, no 2 k156, no 3 k157, no 4 k158 and no 5 k159
quatuor pascal

2112   mozart string quartets no 6 k160, no 7 k168, no 8 k169, no 9 k170 and no 10 k171
quatuor pascal

2113   mozart string quartets no 11 k172, no 12 k173 and no 13 k287
quatuor pascal

2114   mozart string quartets no 14 k421, no 15 k428 and no 16 k458
quatuor pascal

2115   mozart string quartets no 17 k464 and no 18 k465
quatuor pascal
further issue: 2459 (no 17)

2116   mozart string quartets no 19 k499 and no 20 k575
quatuor pascal
further issue: 2459 (no 19)

2117   mozart string quartets no 21 k589 and no 22 k590
quatuor pascal

2118   mozart the two piano quartets
quatuor pascal
pina pozzi, piano

2119   debussy la mer; ravel daphnis et chloe, second suite from the ballet; ravel pavane pour une infante defunte
orchestre du theatre national de l'opera
pierre-michel le conte, conductor
further issues: 591 (pavane), 2583 (daphnis) and 2938 (daphnis)

2120   beethoven fidelio
sinfonieorchester und chor des norddeutschen rundfunks
carl bamberger, conductor
gladys kuchta and melitta muszely, sopranos
julius patzak and helmut kretschmar, tenors
heinz rehfuss, baritone
karl kümmel and erich wenk, basses
further issues: 6231 in set of beethoven stage works, discophilia 28-29
and nonesuch HB 73005
cd: gala GL 100 772
excerpts from the recording also on 945, 2662 and 5012 and 5022 in set 5010-5022

2121 (3-lp) mozart don giovanni
recorded in 1958
badische staatskapelle and chorus
alexander krannhals, conductor
uta graf, elizabeth kingdom and mattiwilda dobbs, sopranos
jean gireaudeau, tenor
paolo gorin and hans hoffmann, baritones
scipio colombo and fritz ollendorff, basses
further issue: festival CFC 60005
excerpts from the recording also on 2492, 5011 in set 5010-5022 and 5221-5222

2122 berlioz symphonie fantastique
orchestre du theatre national de l'opera
pierre-michel le conte, conductor
further issue: 5029

2124 beethoven violin concerto in d op 61
sinfonieorchester des hessischen rundfunks
alexander krannhals, conductor
manoug parikian, violin
also issued in a 6-lp set but using same catalogue number

2125 beethoven piano sonatas no 14, 20 and 23
philippe entremont, piano
further issues: 972 (no 14), 6003 in set 6001-6013 (no 14) and
6103 in set 6101-6112 (no 14)

2131 chopin the fourteen valses
sondra bianca, piano
valse no 6 also on 6006 in set 6001-6013

**2134 johann strauss: g'schichten aus dem wienerwald;
leichtes blut; wiener blut; annen polka; radetzky march;
tritsch-tratsch polka; künstlerleben; perpetuum mobile;
rosen aus dem süden; wein weib und gesang**
recorded in the konzerthaus vienna
wiener symphoniker
gerd heidger, conductor
tritsch-tratsch polka and künstlerleben also on 2297
orchestra described on this recording as vienna festival orchestra

2135   verdi aida, scenes from the opera
orchester der oper frankfurt
carl bamberger, conductor
elizabeth kingdom, soprano
rosl zapf, mezzo-soprano
arturo sergi, tenor
ernst gutstein, bass
orchestral prelude from this recording also on 6111 in set 6101-6112 and 6211

**2136   schumann symphony no 4 in d minor and
genoveva overture**
sinfonieorchester des hessischen rundfunks
otto ackermann, conductor

2138   schubert symphonies no 1 d82 and no 5 d485
sinfonieorchester des hessischen rundfunks
david josefowitz, conductor

**2139   orchestral works by schubert
symphony no 4 d417 "tragic"**
recorded in february 1959 in the town hall wembley
london philharmonic orchestra
sir adrian boult, conductor
further issues: 2248, 2462, 2942, 5206-5207 and
perfect (usa) 15010/13010
rosamunde, suite from the incidental music
orchestre pasdeloup
carl bamberger, conductor
further issues: 956, 3068 in 6-lp set, 5217-5218 (overture) and
6275 in set 6270-6279

2140   beethoven piano trios nos 4 and 7 "archduke"
trio santoliquido
further issue: 2736 (archduke)
cd: pristine audio PASC 058

2141   beethoven piano trios nos 1 and 3
trio santoliquido

2142   beethoven piano trios nos 2 and 9

trio santoliquido

2143   beethoven piano trios nos 5 "ghost" and 6
trio santoliquido
cd: pristine audio PACM 044 (no 6)

2144   **beethoven piano trios nos 8 and 10 and variations on "ich bin der schneider kakadu"**
trio santoliquido

2145   see 2061

2146   **gounod faust ballet music; bizet suites from l'arlesienne and la jolie fille de perth**
orchestre pasdeloup
orchestre des concerts de paris (jolie fille de perth)
walter goehr, conductor

2147   **wagner tannhäuser overture and entry of the guests, fliegende holländer overture and götterdämmerung dawn, rhine journey and funeral music**
badische staatskapelle and chorus
carl bamberger, conductor
sailrs' chorus from fliegende holländer presumably also recorded at these sessions but only issued on 5014 in set 5010-5022

2148   **bach violin concerti nos 1&2 and sonata for violin & cello**
badische staatskapelle
alexander krannhals, conductor
manoug parikian, violin
herbert hoffmann, cello

2149   **mozart piano concerti nos 20 k466 and 23 k488**
sinfonieorchester des hessischen rundfunks
jean entremont, conductor
philippe entremont, piano
further issues: 6101 in set 6101-6112 (no 23) and
festival classique FC 470

2150   **handel music for the royal fireworks and 2 oboe concerti**
frankfurter kammerorchester
gerd heidger, conductor
friedrich plath, oboe

2151   **ballet music by delibes**
coppelia and sylvia   see 216
la source
orchestre des concerts de paris
georg walter, conductor
further issue: 6438 in set 6436-6441

2152   **brahms piano concerto no 2 in b flat op 83**

recorded in hilversum
amsterdam philharmonic society
walter goehr, conductor
ventsislav yankoff, piano

2153 (3-lp) handel messiah, oratorio

recorded in hilversum
handel society orchestra and chorus
walter goehr, conductor
mattiwilda dobbs, soprano
grace hoffman, contralto
leopold simoneau, tenor
heinz rehfuss, baritone
excerpts from the recording also on 522 and 3051

2155   **tchaikovsky symphony no 5 in e minor op 64**

rai roma orchestra
walter goehr, conductor
further issues: 6013 in set 6001-6013 and 6108 in set 6101-6112

2156   **tchaikovsky swan lake and sleeping beauty, suites**

orchestra dell' opera di roma
walter goehr, conductor
further issue: 3047
this was possibly the first lp to be published in the synchro-stereo format

2157 (3-lp) verdi aida

recorded in 1958 in rome
orchestra e coro dell' opera di roma
ernesto barbini, conductor
anna de cavalieri, soprano
ira malaniuk, contralto
aldo bertocci, tenor
scipio colombo, baritone
paolo dari and ugo trama, basses
further issue: 6331-6333 in 6-lp set of verdi opras
excerpts from the recording also on 2926, 3053 and 5017 in set 5010-5022

2158 (2-lp) donizetti lucia di lammermoor

recorded in 1958 in rome
orchestra e coro dell' opera di roma
alberto paoletti, conductor
margherita rinaldi, soprano
enzo tei and vito tatone, tenors
giovanni pica, baritone
sergio ballani, bass
excerpts from the recording also on 2924 and 5014 in set 5010-5022

2159   works by beethoven
triple concerto
rai roma orchestra
walter goehr, conductor
ornella santoliquido, piano
manoug parikian, violin
massimo amfitheatrof, cello
twelve german dances   see 10

2161   symphonies by haydn
symphony no 104 "london"
recorded between 23-27 february 1959 in the town hall wembley
london philharmonic orchestra
sir adrian boult, conductor
further issues: 2910, 5008, in 6-lp set, classics club X 86 and
perfect (usa) 13003/15003
cd: trax classique TRXCD 134
symphony no 101 "clock"   see 2088

2164   vivaldi le 4 stagioni and violin concerto in e minor
frankfurter kammerorchester
david josefowitz, conductor
saschko gavriloff, violin
further issue: 6270 in set 6270-6279

2166   orchestral works by dvorak
serenade for strings
boyd neel orchestra
boyd neel, conductor
czech suite
amsterdam philharmonic society
walter goehr, conductor

2167 (2-lp)   vivaldi l'estro armonico op 3
frankfurter kammerorchester
walter goehr, conductor
saschko gavriloff, violin
selection from the concerti also on 2560

2168   overtures by french composers
pierre-michel le conte, conductor
berlioz benvenuto cellini
orchestre de l'opera de paris
**auber fra diavolo and le cheval de bronze; lalo le roi d'ys;
boildieu le caliphe de bagdad and la dame blanche**
orchestre des concerts de paris
further issues: 2197 and 2911
2197 contained herold zampa in place of lalo le roi d'ys

2169   overtures and scenes from operas by bellini
rai roma orchestra
ferruccio scaglia, conductor
fiorella ortis, soprano
salvatore gioia, tenor
selection from the recordings also on 5013 in set 5010-5022

**2172 (2-lp)   symphonies by beethoven
symphony no 9 in d minor op 125 "choral"**
sinfonieorchester des hessischen rundfunks
frankfurter cäcilienverein
walter goehr, conductor
agnes giebel, soprano
marga höffgen, contralto
helmut krebs, tenor
fritz ollendorff, bass
further issues: 2245 and 5009
symphony no 8 in f op 93   see 197

2173   see 221

2174   orchestral works by ravel and chabrier
espana and suite pastorale
orchestre des concerts de paris
pierre-michel le conte, conductor
la valse and rapsodie espagnole   see 203 and 217

2175   works by twentieth century composers
schoenberg serenade op 24
recorded in december 1949 in new york
contemporary music society ensemble
dimitri mitropoulos, conductor
warren galjour, baritone
further issues: counterpoint esoteric CPT 501/5501S/MC 20005
bartok divertimento
zimbler sinfonietta
lukas foss, conductor

2176   recital of organ works by bach

pierre cochereau, organ

2177   recital of organ works by bach-liszt, calviere, franck, mendelssohn, frescobaldi and widor
pierre cochereau, organ

2178   recital of piano music by schubert
lili kraus, piano
valses sentimentales
further issues: 517 and 5313-5214
moments musicaux nos 2 and 3
further issues: 517, 946 (no 2), 2726 and 6413
piano sonata no 20 in a d959; ländler d366; ecossaises d145

2179   concerti by haydn
cello concerto in d
orchester der wiener staatsoper
hans swarowsky, conductor
aldo parisot, cello
violin concerto in g
radio geneva orchestra
pierre colombo, conductor
saschko gavriloff, violin
further issue: 2230
both works also issued in a 6-lp set but retaining same catalogue number

2180   cantatas by bach
wiener kammerorchester
wiener akademiechor
felix prohaska, conductor
cantata no 140 "wachet auf ruft uns die stimme"
anny felbermayer, soprano
alfred uhl, tenor
hans braun, baritone
cantata no 4 "christ lag in todesbanden"

2182 (2-lp)   bach mass in b minor
recorded in hilversum
amsterdam philharmonic society orchestra and chorus
walter goehr, conductor
pierrette alarie and catherine delfosse, sopranos
grace hoffman, contralto
leopold simoneau, tenor
heinz rehfuss, baritone
further issue: vanguard SRV 216-217

2183   mozart concert arias and operatic duets from idomeneo,
entführung aus dem serail, cosi fan tutte and la finta giardiniera
recorded in hilversum
amsterdam philharmonic society
walter goehr, conductor
pierrette alarie, soprano
leopold simoneau, tenor
further issue: pearl SHE 573

2184 (3-lp)   bizet carmen

recorded in 1959 in paris
orchestre et choeurs des concerts de paris
pierre-michel le conte, conductor
consuelo rubio, mezzo-soprano
pierette alarie, soprano
leopold simoneau, tenor
heinz rehfuss, baritone
further issues: 6300-6302 in 6-lp set of french opera and
epic (usa) SC 6035 and BSC 106
cd: hamburger archiv für gesangskunst 30045
*excerpts from the recording also on 532, 957, 967, 2409, 5019 in set 5010-5022,
6111, 6211, 6300, 7025 and 7027*

**2186   waltzes and polkas from vienna
johann strauss frühlingsstimmen; morgenblätter; du und du;
freikugeln; accelerationen; josef strauss ohne sorgen;
vergnügungszug; sphärenklänge; johann and josef
pizzicato polka**
orchester der wiener staatsoper
hans swarowsky, conductor
selection from the recordings also on 6108 in set 6101-6113 and 7028

**2187   lieder aus der jugendzeit: orchestral arrangements of
songs by schumann, schubert, liszt, beethoven, silcher, mozart
and wolf/**vanguard recording
orchester der wiener staatsoper
anton paulik, conductor
erich kunz, baritone
vanguard issue: SRV 477
further issues: philips A04304L and 838 204AY

2188   works by tchaikovsky
serenade for strings
frankfurter kammerorchester
walter goehr, conductor
further issue: 3048
rococo variations for cello and orchestra
orchester der wiener staatsoper
pierre-michel le conte, conductor
aldo parisot, cello
further issues: 950, 3046 and 3049

2189   works by liszt and johann strauss: hungarian
rhapsodies nos 1, 2, 3 and 6 & czardas from ritter pasman
orchester der wiener staatsoper
hans swarowsky, conductor
further issues: 5219-5220 (hungarian rhapsody no 6 & czardas)
and 6107 in set 6101-6112 (hungarian rhapsodies nos 2 & 3)
cd: pristine audio PASC 159 (hungarian rhapsody no 2)

2190   concerti by schumann
piano concerto in a minor
orchester der wiener staatsoper
victor desarzens, conductor
lili kraus, piano
further issues: 2327, 3077, 6005 in set 6001-6013, 6107 in set
6101-6112 and 6206 in set 6201-6212, festival classique FC 428
and vanguard SRV 293
cd: scribendum SC 018
cello concerto   see 228

2191   works by mozart
lili kraus, piano
piano concerto no 9 in e flat k271
orchester der wiener staatsoper
victor desarzens, conductor
further issues: 2912 and festival classique FC 423
cd: scribendum SC 018
piano sonata no 11 in a k331
further issues: 534, 2912 and festival classique FC 423

2192   **works for piano and orchestra by beethoven**
orchester der wiener staatsoper
victor desarzens, conductor
lili kraus, piano
piano concerto no 4 in g op 58
further issues: 2294, vanguard SRV 252 and prestige de la musique SR 9613
cd: scribendum SC 018 and ages 509 0042
rondo in b flat for piano and orchestra
further issues: vanguard SRV 252 and prestige de la musique SR 9613
cd: ages 509 0042

2193   **brahms liebeslieder walzer and neue liebeslieder**
walzer/rias berlin recording
erna berger, soprano
gertrude pitzinger, contralto
walther ludwig, tenor
erich wenk, bass
ernst-günter scherzer and gerda falbe, pianos
further issue: quadriga 1005 703.704
cd: fnac music 642 313

2197   see 2168
2198   see 2173

2199   **benatzky im weissen rössl and lehar paganini,**
scenes from the operettas sung in french
orchestre des concerts de paris
andre gallois, conductor
suzanne auret, soprano
remy corazza, tenor
emile peters, baritone

2200   **lecocq la fille de madame angot and planquette**
les cloches de corneville, scenes from the operettas
orchestre des concerts de paris
andre gallois, conductor
suzanne auret and liliane berton, sopranos
remy corazza, tenor
emile peters, baritone
further issue: 2449
excerpts from la fille de madame angot also on 5020 in set 5010-5022

2201   symphonies by beethoven
walter goehr, conductor
symphony no 5 in c minor op 67
recorded on 25-26 july 1958 in the town hall watford
london symphony orchestra
further issues: 5003, 5004, 6002 in set 6001-6013
and perfect (usa) 13004/15004
symphony no 1 in c op 21   see 219

**2202   benatzky im weissen rössl & zeller der vogelhändler,
scenes from the operettas**
wiener operettenorchester
georg walter, conductor
ingeborg fanger, hilde breyer and edith berg, sopranos
reinhold günter and kurt wolinski, tenors
gottlieb zeithammer, baritone

2203   schubert trout quintet and quartettsatz d703
quatuor pascal
vlado perlemuter, piano
also issued in 6-lp set using same catalogue number

**2204   overtures by rossini: la scala di seta, semiramide,
la cenerentola, il barbiere di siviglia, l'italiana in algeri,
il signor bruschino and tancredi**
radio geneva orchestra
gianfranco rivoli, conductor
further issues: 997 (barbiere and italiana) and 2734 (barbiere)

**2205   mendelssohn violin concerto in e minor and
paganini violin concerto no 1**
recorded in 1954
radio geneva orchestra
gianfranco rivoli, conductor
ricardo odnoposoff, violin
further issue: 3066 (mendelssohn)
cd: doremi DHR 7874-7879

2206   mozart violin concerti no 1 k207 and no 5 k219
orchestre des concerts colonne (no 1)
amsterdam philharmonic society (no 5)
walter goehr, conductor
manoug parikian, violin

2207   chopin 24 preludes op 28 and prelude op 45
vlado perlemuter, piano

2208   brahms symphony no 2 in d op 73 and academic academic festival overture
recorded in may-june 1960 in geneva
tonhalle-orchester zürich
josef krips, conductor
further issue: festival classique FC 450
cd: ages 509.0062 (symphony only) and ades 13.2742

2209 (2-lp)   haydn die schöpfung
orchester der wiener staatsoper
wiener akademiechor
walter goehr, conductor
agnes giebel, soprano
richard holm, tenor
heinz rehfuss, baritone
further issue: 6376-6377 in set 6376-6381

2210   recital of organ works by bach
recorded in the enge-kirche zürich
erich vollenwyder, organ
also issued in a 6-lp set retaining the same catalogue number

2211   overtures by suppe: die schöne galathea; dichter und bauer; banditenstreiche; leichte kavallerie; boccaccio; morgen mittag und abend in wien
orchester der wiener staatsoper
walter goehr, conductor

2212   russian orchestral music khachaturian gayaneh suite and kabalevsky the comedians
orchester der wiener staatsoper
vladimir golschmann, conductor
rimsky-korsakov introduction and march from le coq d'or
see CHS 1106

2214   mendelssohn a midsummer night's dream, incidental music; hebrides overture
recorded in 1960 in baden-baden
sinfonieorchester des südwestfunks
carl schuricht, conductor
further issues: 968 (dream), 2734 (hebrides), 5211-5212 (hebrides), 5217-5218 (dream), 5225 (hebrides), 7027 (hebrides) and columbia (japan) OW 7878
cd: denon (japan) 30CO 1342 and scribendum SC 011

2215   schubert symphony no 9 d944 "great"
recorded in september 1960 in the sdr studios stuttgart
sinfonieorchester des süddeutschen rundfunks
carl schuricht, conductor
further issues: 2729, vanguard SRV 218, prestige SR 9658,
columbia (japan) OW 7883, festival classique FC 427 and in
multiple commemorative lp set for carl schuricht
cd: columbia (japan) COCO 6587, theorema THS 12 1172
and scribendum SC 011
also issued in 6-lp set bur retaining same catalogue number

2216   tchaikovsky symphony no 6 op 74 "pathetique"
recorded in october 1960 in the tonhalle zürich
tonhalle-orchester zürich
josef krips, conductor
further issues: 5035, 5006-5007, 5031-5032, accord 140 071
and festival classique FC 432
also issued in 6-lp set but retaining same catalogue number

**2217   schumann symphony no 3 "rhenish" and
manfred overture**
recorded in december 1960 in the sdr studios stuttgart
sinfonieorchester des süddeutschen rundfunks
carl schuricht, conductor
further issues: 5008 (symphony) and columbia (japan) OW 7879
cd: scribendum SC 011
also issued in 6-lp set but retaining same catalogue number

**2218   operatic overtures by mozart: le nozze di figaro, don
giovanni, die zauberflöte, die entführung aus dem serail, la
clemenza di tito, cosi fan tutte, la finta giardiniera and idomeneo**
recorded in december 1960 in the tonhalle zürich
tonhalle-orchester zürich
josef krips, conductor
further issue: festival classique FC 456
*figaro overture also issued on 957, 967, 2734, 5022 in set 5010-5022,
6211 and 7027; complete record also issued in a 6-lp set but retaining
same catalogue number*

2219   schubert octet
quatuor pascal
jacques lancelot, clarinet
paul hongue, bassoon
gilbert cousier, horn
gaston longerot, double-bass

2220   **beethoven septet**
members of quatuor pascal
jacques lancelot, clarinet
paul hongue, bassoon
gilbert cousier, horn
gaston longerot, double-bass
further issue: 6246 in 6-lp set

2221   **beethoven piano sonatas nos 8, 19 and 21**
lili kraus, piano
further issues: 6236 (no 8), 6239 (no 19), 6240 (no 21)
and festival classique FC 403
cd: ages 509 0042 (nos 19 and 21)
6236, 6239 and 6240 formed part of a multiple set of the complete
beethoven piano sonatas

2222   **beethoven violin sonatas op 24 "spring"**
and op 47 "kreutzer"
manoug parikian, violin
magda tagliaferro, piano

2223   **recital of piano music by chopin**

vlado perlemuter, piano

2224   **dvorak symphony no 9 op 95 "new world"**
recorded in october 1960 in the tonhalle zürich
tonhalle-orchester zürich
josef krips, conductor
further issues: 5006-5007, 5033, 6209 in set 6201-6212 and
festival classique FC 409
also issued in a 6-lp set but retaining the same catalogue number and on
cd in america on the rediscovery label

2225   **music for violin and piano by vieuxtemps,**
wieniawski, leclair, tchaikovsky, zarzycki, paganini and
szymanowski/melodiya recording
david oistrakh, violin
vladimir yampolsky, piano
taken from melodiya originals recorded between 1945-1953 and also issued
on lp by monarch, period, chant du monde and others

2226   this was a duplication of 2225, except that a piece by
sarasate replaced the one by szymanowski

2227 (2-lp)   verdi la traviata
recorded in 1960 in the konzerthaus vienna
orchester und chr der wiener staatsoper
gianfranco rivoli, conductor
elena todeschi, soprano
augusto vicentini, tenor
renato cesari, baritone
further issues: in 6-lp set of verdi operas but retaining same
catalogue number and festival classique CFC 60007
excerpts from the recording also on 2353 and 5017 in set 5010-5022

2228 (2-lp) messager veronique
orchestre et choeurs des concerts de paris
andre gallois, conductor
liliane berton and suzanne aurat, sopranos
remy corazza, tenor
emile peters, baritone
excerpts from the recording also on 2397. 2476 and 7025

2230   see 211 and 2179

2231   **bach orchestral suites nos 2 and 3**
recorded in 1961 in the studios of hessischer rundfunk
sinfonieorchester des hessischen rundfunks
carl schuricht, conductor
further issues: 6271 in set 6270-6279 (suite no 2), in a 6-lp set
retaining same catalogue number and columbia (japan) OW 7881

2232   **kalman die czardasfürstin, scenes from the operetta**
wiener operettenorchester und –chor
boris mersson, conductor
gerry grosz and hea reuss, sopranos
fred bongers, tenor
franz müller, baritone
excerpts from the recording also on 2386, 2476, 7017 and 7125

2233   **dvorak slavonic dances op 46 and op 72, selection**
recorded in july 1961 in the maison de la radio paris
orchestre national
paul kletzki, conductor
further issue: in 6-lp set retaining same catalogue number
*excerpts from the recording also on 993, 2297, 2548, 5219-5220, 6411,
7026 and emi cd 575 4682*

2234   adam giselle, scenes from the ballet

orchestre des concerts de paris
gianfranco rivoli, conductor
further issue: 5203 and in 12-lp set of ballet music
excerpts from the recording also on 2760, 5203-5204, 6409 and 7022

2235   symphonies by mendelssohn
symphony no 1
orchestre du theatre national de l'opera
david josefowitz, conductor
symphony no 4 "italian"   see 218

2236   beethoven piano concerto no 3 & choral fantasy
recorded in hilversum
orchestra and chorus of the amsterdam philharmonic society
gianfranco rivoli, conductor
lili kraus, piano
further issue: 2285 (concerto) and in 6-lp set of beethoven concerti
cd: scribendum SC 018

2237   tchaikovsky casse noisette, scenes from the ballet
recorded in hilversum
amsterdam philharmonic society
gianfranco rivoli, conductor
further issues: in 6-lp and 12-lp sets retaining same catalogue number
*excerpts from the recording also on 500, 594, 3047, 5203-5204, 6208 in set
6201-6212, 6409 and 7021 in set 7021-7029*

2238 (3-lp) operas by mascagni and leoncavallo/cetra recordings
recorded in 1951-1952 in turin
rai torino orchestra and chorus
cavalleria rusticana
arturo basile, conductor
giulietta simionato, mezzo-soprano
liliana pellegrino, soprano
achille braschi, tenor
carlo tagliabue, bass
cetra issues: LPC 1233, LPS 3233, OLPC 1238 and CS 558-559
cd: cetra DOC 27 and fonit 8573 872712
i pagliacci
alfredo simonetto, conductor
carla cavazzi, soprano
carlo bergonzi, tenor
marcello rossi, baritone
carlo tagliabue, bass
cetra issues: LPO 2024, LPC 1227, OLPC 1238 and CS 527-528
cd: cetra DOC 27 and fonit 8573 872712
excerpts from the recordings also on 5020 in set 5010-5022, 6406 and 7025

2239   **beethoven symphony no 6 in f op 68 "pastoral"**
recorded in the maison de la radio paris
orchestre national
paul kletzki, conductor
further issues: 6202 and festival classique FC 402
excerpts from the recording also on 5209-5210

2240   **bach cantatas nos 80 and 104**
recorded in hilversum
amsterdam philharmonic society and bach choir
andre vandernoot, conductor
agnes giebel, soprano (no 80 only)
wilhelmine matthes, contralto (no 80 only)
richard lewis, tenor
heinz rehfuss, baritone
further issue: vanguard SRV 219

2241   **tchaikovsky symphony no 4 in f minor op 36**
recorded in the maison de la radio paris
orchestre national
paul kletzki, conductor

2242 (3-lp) bach johannes-passion
recorded in hilversum
amsterdam philharmonic society and bach choir
andre vandernoot, conductor
agnes giebel, soprano
wilhelmine matthes, contralto
richard lewis, tenor
heinz rehfuss, baritone
further issue: nonesuch HB 73004
excerpts from the recording also on 2765

2243   **mozart piano concerti nos 19 k459 & 26 k537**
recorded in hilversum
amsterdam philharmonic society
gianfranco rivoli, conductor
lili kraus, piano
further issues: 2726 (no 26), 2944 (no 26) and festival
classique FC 455 (no 26)
cd: scribendum SC 018 (both) and preludio PHC 1131 (no 26)

2244   recital of lieder by schubert, schumann, brahms and wolf
heinz rehfuss, baritone
frank martin, piano

2245   see 2172

2246   orchestral music by wagner: rienzi overture, siegfried idyll, lohengrin prelude and suite from meistesinger
recorded in september 1961 in the herkulessaal munich
sinfonieorchester des bayerischen rundfunks
carl schuricht, conductor
further issues: in multiple commemorative lp set for carl schuricht (all works), 2548 (lohengrin), 5022 in set 5010-5022 (meistersinger), 6277 in set 6270-6279 (lohengrin) and vanguard SRV 220 (all works)
cd: denon (japan) 30CO 1340 and scribendum SC 011

2248   see 218 and 2139

2249   brahms symphony no 4 in e minor and tragic overture
recorded in september 1961 in the herkulessaal munich
sinfonieorchester des bayerischen rundfunks
carl schuricht, conductor
further issues: 5005 (symphony), 5031 (symphony), in 6-lp set retaining same catalogue number, in multiple commemorative lp set for carl schuricht, columbia (japan) OW 7314 and festival classique FC 405
cd: denon (japan) 30CO 1337, ades 13.2782, scribendum SC 011 and ages 509.0022 (symphony)

2250   works for violin and orchestra: saint-saens introduction and rondo capriccioso and havanaise, sarasate zigeunerweisen and chausson poeme
recorded in 1955
radio geneva orchestra
gianfranco rivoli, conductor
ricardo odnoposoff, violin
further issues: 537 (zigeunerweisen) and 7026 (zigeunerweisen)
cd: doremi DHR 7874-7879

2251 **schubert piano sonata no 15, moment musical no 3,
allegretto in c minor and four ländler/**chant du monde recording
recorded on 19-20 october 1961 in paris
sviatoslav richter, piano
chant du monde issues: LDX 7943, LDX 8295 and LDXS 78295
further issues: hall of fame HOF 528/HOFS 528, monitor
MC 2057/MCS 2057, melodiya D 011755-011756/M10 11755 007
cd: monitor 55.008
selection from the recording also on 965

2252 **mozart german dances k509, k602 and k605,
march k408 and gavotte k300/**philips recording
recorded on 16-17 june 1955 in the mozarteum salzburg
camerata academica salzburg
bernhard paumgartner, conductor
philips issue: A00374L
selection from the recording also on 971 and 5219-5220

2253 see 76, 217 and 2174

2257 **bach concerti in a and in f minor, fantasy
in c minor and italian concerto**
radio geneva chamber orchestra
pierre colombo, conductor
isabelle nef, harpsichord

2258 **symphonies by mozart**
orchestre du theatre de l'opera
carl schuricht, conductor
symphony no 36 in c k425 "linz"
recorded in november 1964 in paris
further issues: in 6-lp set retaining same catalogue number, in
multiple commemorative lp set for carl schuricht and
festival classique FC 420
cd: denon (japan) 30CO 1336 and ades 13.2292
symphony no 40 in g minor k550
recorded in june 1964 in paris
further issues: 6202 in set 6201-6212, in 6-lp set retaining same
catalogue number, in multiple commemorative lp set for carl
schuricht and festival classique FC 420
cd: denon (japan) 30CO 1335, ades 13.2292 and scribendum SC 011

2259   **giordano andrea chenier, scenes**/cetra recording
recorded in 1953 in turin
rai torino orchestra and chorus
arturo basile, conductor
renata tebaldi, soprano
irma colasanti, mezzo-soprano
jose soler, tenor
ugo savarese, baritone
excerpts from the rcording also on 5021 in set 5010-5022; complete opera
published on the cetra, fonit, everest and deutsche grammophon labels

2263   **kalman die czardasfürstin, scenes sung in french**
orchestre et choeur des concerts de paris
boris mersson, conductor
andrea guiot, soprano
helene sury, mezzo-soprano
remy corazza, tenor
francois meunier, baritone

2266   **handel concerto in c "alexander's feast" and concerti grossi op 3 no 6 and op 6 nos 4 and 10**
recorded in september 1961 in the herkulessaal munich
sinfonieorchester des bayerischen rundfunks
carl schuricht, conductor
further issues: in multiple commemorative lp set for carl schuricht
and columbia (japan) OW 7882
cd: scribendum SC 011

2268   **brahms symphony no 1 in c minor op 68**
recorded in june 1962 in the konzerthaus vienna
wiener symphoniker
josef krips, conductor
further issue: in 6-lp set but retaining same catalogue number and
vanguard SRV 221
orchestra described on this recording as vienna festival orchestra

2269   **mahler symphony no 1 in d "titan"**
recorded in may 1962 in the konzerthaus vienna
wiener symphoniker
willem van otterloo, conductor
orchestra described on this recording as vienna festival orchestra

2270   **beethoven piano concerto no 5 & ruinen von athen overture**
recorded in the konzerthaus vienna
wiener symphoniker
christian voechting, conductor
vlado perlemuter, piano
further issues: 3060, 6003 and 6103 in set 6101-6112 (concerto)
orchestra described on this recording as vienna festival orchestra

2271   **johann strauss an der schönen blauen donau; i tipferl;**
die fledermaus overture; kaiserwalzer; march from der
zigeunerbaron; waldmeister overture
recorded in september 1962 in the konzerthaus vienna
wiener symphoniker
josef krips, conductor
further issue: festival classique FC 429
selections from the recordings on 514, 979, 2548, 2684, 2685, 5213-5214,
6210 in set 6201-6212 and 7028; orchestra described on this recording as
vienna festival orchestra

2272   **concertante works by mozart**
sinfonia concertante k364/melodiya recording
moscow chamber orchestra
rudolf barshai, conductor and viola
david oistrakh, violin
melodiya issue: D 05236-05237
further issues: 2291, artia ALP 165, musidisc RC 059, period
SHO 343/SHOST 343, vedette VSC 4020, eurodisc ZK 77293,
recital hall RH 301 and chant du monde LDP 8248/LDX 78698
cd: chant du monde LDC 278 096
sinfonia concertante k297b
orchestre du theatre de l'opera
david josefowitz, conductor
lucien debray, oboe
jacques lancelot, clarinet
maurice allard, bassoon
lucien thevet, horn

2273   **liszt: paganini etudes nos 5 and 6; hungarian rhapsody no 9;**
legend no 2; consolation no 3; liebestraum no 3; petrarch sonnet 123
bela siki, piano
further issues: 5222 (liebestraum) and 6415 (etude no 5, hungarian rhapsody,
consolation and liebestraum)

2274   overtures by beethoven: fidelio, egmont, coriolan, leonore no 3 and die weihe des hauses
recorded in september 1962 in the konzerthaus vienna
wiener symphoniker
josef krips, conductor
further issues: 512 (fidelio and coriolan), 2695 (coriolan, leonore no 3 and weihe), 5217-5218 (egmont), 5225 (leonore no 3), 6220 (leonore no 3 and weihe) and 6273 in st 6270-6279 (all works)
cd: preludio PHS 1123
orchestra described on this recording as vienna festival orchestra

2275   beethoven symphony no 3 in e flat op 55 "eroica"
sinfonieorchester des südwestfunks
paul kletzki, conductor
further issue: in 7-lp set of beethoven symphonies but retaining same catalogue number

2276   rimsky-korsakov scheherazade, symphonic suite
recorded in may-june 1963 in the konzerthaus vienna
wiener symphoniker
willem van otterloo, conductor
further issues: 7023 and festival classique FC 426
cd: fnac musique 642 330
excerpts from the recording also on 5201-5202; orchestra described on this recording as vienna festival orchestra

2277   grieg peer gynt, first and second suites from the from the incidental music and 4 norwegian dances
recorded in the konzerthaus vienna
wiener symphoniker
gianfranco rivoli, conductor
selections from the recording on 508, 2760, 5211-5212, 5217-5218, 6206 in set 6201-6212, 6407, 6408, 7022 and on cd in america on the rediscovery label; orchestra described on this recording as vienna festival orchestra

2279   brahms the complete hungarian dances
recorded in the konzerthaus vienna
wiener symphoniker
david josefowitz, conductor
further issue: in 6-lp set but retaining same catalogue number
selections from the recording on 506, 2297, 5219-5220 and 7026; orchestra described on this recording as vienna festival orchestra

2280   see CH-E14 and 208

2281   sibelius symphony no 2 in d op 43
recorded in the konzerthaus vienna
wiener symphoniker
christian voechting, conductor
orchestra described on this recording as vienna festival orchestra

2282 (3-lp)   gounod faust
recorded in 1957 in the konzerthaus vienna
orchester und chor der wiener staatsoper
gianfranco rivoli, conductor
pierrette alarie and liliane berton, sopranos
leopold simoneau, tenor
heinz rehfuss, baritone
further issues: 2374, 6302-6305 in set 6300-6305 and festival
classique CFC 60082
cd: fnac 642 314 and vai audio 1143
excerpts from the recording also on 5018 in set 5010-5022

2283   beethoven symphony no 7 & könig stephan overture
recorded in may 1962 in the konzerthaus vienna
wiener symphoniker
willem van otterloo, conductor
further issue: in 7-lp set of beethoven symphonies but retaining
same catalogue number
orchestra described on this recording as vienna festival orchestra

2284   works by brahms
recorded in september 1962 in baden-baden
sinfonieorchester des südwestfunks
carl schuricht, conductor
symphony no 3 in f op 90
further issue: festival classique FC 469
cd: denon (japan) 30CO 1338 and ages 509 0022
variations on a theme of haydn
further issues: 3075 and festival classique FC 469
cd: denon (japan) 30CO 1338 and scribendum SC 011

2285   see 2236

2286 (2-lp) puccini tosca/cetra recording
recorded in 1955 in turin
rai torino orchestra and chorus
arturo basile, conductor
gigliola frazzoni, soprano
ferruccio tagliavini, tenor
giangiacomo guelfi, baritone
cetra issues: LPS 3261 and OLPC 1261
further issues: 6316-6317 in 6-lp set of puccini operas and
balkanton BOA 1573-1574
cd: cetra CDO 500 and fonit 8573 874792
excerpts from the recording also on 2413, 5021 in set 5010-5022 and 7025

2287 brahms violin concerto in d op 77/melodiya recording
recorded in 1952 in moscow
ussr large radio orchestra
kyrill kondrashin, conductor
david oistrakh, violin
melodiya 78rpm issue: D 021869-021877
melodiya lp issue: D 0857-0858/D 07387-07388
further issue: 6009 in set 6001-6013
cd: melodiya CD10 00745/CD10 00741, rca bmg 74321 341792/
74321 407102 and urania URN 22233
also issued on the colosseum, bruno, hall of fame, period, monarch, musidisc,
vanguard, chant du monde, vox, murray hill, telefunken, saga, eurodisc,
westminster, supraphon and dante labels

2288 see CHS 1155 and 209
2291 see 2272 and 2291

2292 (2-lp) the beggars' opera
max goberman, conductor
mary thomas and doreen murray, sopranos
jean allister, contralto
william mcalpine, tenor
ronald lewis, baritone

2293 overtures by german romantic composers
nicolai die lustigen weiber von windsor, weber oberon and
mendelssohn ruy blas see 225
weber euryanthe and mendelssohn die schöne melusine
recorded in september 1962 in baden-baden
sinfonieorchester des südwestfunks
carl schuricht, conductor
further issues: 5201-5202 (schöne melusine), in multiple commemorative
lp set for carl schuricht and columbia (japan) OW 7884
cd: scribendum SC 011 (schöne melusine)

2294   see 10 and 2192

2295   **stravinsky apollon musagete & roussel sinfonietta**
ramat gan chamber orchestra
sergiu commissiona, conductor
abraham comfort, violin

2296   **albinoni sonata a cinque op 5 no 9 and concerto
for strings op 7 no 1; boccherini symphony no 1 op 3;
corelli suite for strings; tartini sinfonia in d**
ramat gan chamber orchestra
sergiu commissiona, conductor
further issue: 509 (albinoni op 5 no 9 and corelli)

2298   **recital of works for cello and piano
mendelssohn variations concertantes op 17; schumann
fantasiestücke op 73 and 5 stücke im volkston; schubert
arpeggione sonata**
pierre fournier, cello
dorel handman, piano
further issues: 3068 (schubert) and 3078 (schumann)

2299   **lobet den herrn: choral and organ works by bach, schröter,
schütz, hassler, bruckner, mozart, arcadet, haydn and buxtehude**
chor der zürcher kantorei
richard haselbach, conductor
hans vollenwyder, organ
elfriede pfleger, soprano

2300   **bartok concerto for orchestra**/mercury recording
recorded on 23-24 december 1953 in the northrop auditorium minneapolis
minneapolis symphony orchestra
antal dorati, conductor
mercury issues: MG 50033, MLP 7526, MRL 2521 and MMA 11082

2302   **oscar straus der letzte walzer, scenes from the operetta**
wiener operettenorchester und –chor
oscar straus, conductor
margit opawski and lieselotte maikl, sopranos
rudolf christ, tenor
norman foster, bass

2303   millöcker der bettelstudent, scenes from the operetta
wiener operettenorchester und –chor
robert stolz, conductor
margit opawski and ruthilde boesch, sopranos
rudolf christ and hugo meyer-welfing, tenors
kurt preger and fritz krenn, basses

2304   stolz zwei herzen im dreivierteltakt, scenes
wiener operettenorchester und –chor
robert stolz, conductor
margit opawski and ruthilde boesch, sopranos
rudolf christ and hugo meyer-welfing, tenors
kurt preger and fritz krenn, basses

2305   oboe concerti by bach and leclair
orchestre de chambre romand
alain milhaud, conductor
heinz holliger, oboe

2306   see HDL 4, HDL 5 and HDL 6

2307   beethoven piano concerto no 5 and piano sonata no 27
recorded in the konzerthaus vienna
orchester der wiener staatsoper
hans swarowsky, conductor
friedrich gulda, piano
further issues: 6003 in set 6001-6013, 6203 in set 6201-6212 (concerto)
and in 6-lp set of beethoven concerti but retaining same catalogue
number
cd: pristine audio PASC 159 (concerto), scribendum SC 016 and
ages 509 0072
pristine audio incorrectly describes pianist as hannes kann

2308   stravinsky petrushka/mercury recording
recorded on 6 april 1955 in the northrop auditorium minneapolis
minneapolis symphony orchestra
antal dorati, conductor
mercury issues: MG 50058, MGW 14038, SRW 18038 and MRL 2523
further issue: philips wing WL 1035
excerpts from the recording also on 531

2309 strauss till eulenspiegels lustige streiche and suite from der rosenkavalier arranged by dorati/mercury recording
recorded on 22 december 1955 in the northrop auditorium minneapolis
minneapolis symphony orchestra
antal dorati, conductor
mercury 45rpm issue: XEP 9033 (till)
mercury lp issues: MG 50099, MG 50334 (till), SR 90099
(rosenkavalier), SR 90334 (till), MGW 14072, MGW 14501
(rosenkavalier), SRW 18072, SRW 18501 (rosenkavalier),
MRL 2566, MMA 11061, AMS 16104, SRI 75016 (rosenkavalier),
121 028MGL (rosenkavalier) and 131 028MGY (rosenkavalier)
other issues: philips classical favourites GL 5831 (till), SGL 5831
(till), 642 270GL (till), 837 879GY (till) and 937 894GY
(rosenkavalier) and philips festivo 839 847GSY (rosenkavalier)
cd: philips mercury 434 3482

2310 recital of keyboard music by bach

vasso devetzi, piano

2312 (2-lp) verdi requiem and te deum/4 pezzi sacri
recorded in the konzerthaus vienna
orchester und chor der wiener staatsoper
gianfranco rivoli, conductor
gloria davy, soprano
suze leal, mezzo-soprano
glade peterson, tenor
heinz rehfuss, baritone
further issues: 2336 and in 6-lp set of choral music

2313 symphonies by beethoven
symphony no 1 in c op 21 see 219
symphony no 5 in c minor op 67
sinfonieorchester des südwestfunks
paul kletzki, conductor
further issues: 2341, 3072-3073, 6202 in set 6201-6212 and
in 6-lp and 7-lp sets but retaining same catalogue number

2314 chopin piano concerto no 2 in f minor and mendelssohn piano concerto no 1 in g minor
recorded in the konzerthaus vienna
orchester der wiener staatsoper
hans swarowsky, conductor
menahem pressler, piano
further issues: 2920 (chopin), 3066 (mendelsshn), 5222 (chopin)
and in 6-lp set retaining same catalogue number

2315   cello concerti by haydn and boccherini
recorded in the konzerthaus vienna
wiener kammerorchester
david josefowitz, conductor
bernard greenhouse, cello

2316   overtures and choruses from verdi operas
recorded in the konzerthaus vienna
orchester und chor der wiener staatsoper
nello santi, conductor

2317   overtures and choruses from german operas
recorded in the konzerthaus vienna
orchester und chor der wiener staatsoper
hans swarowsky, conductor

2318   liszt hungarian rhapsodies nos 2, 5, 6, 12 & 15
recorded in the konzerthaus vienna
orchester der wiener staatsoper
hiroyuki iwaki, conductor
further issue: 5211-5212 (no 2)

2319   mozart piano concerti nos 21 in k467 and 27 k595
recorded in the konzerthaus vienna
orchester der wiener staatsoper
hans swarowsky, conductor
friedrich gulda, piano
further issues: 6201 in set 6201-6212 (no 27), in a 6-lp set retaining
same catalogue number and on the pearl label
cd: scribendum SC 016

2320   dances, contredances and minuets by beethoven
recorded in the konzerthaus vienna
orchester der wiener staatsoper
david josefowitz, conductor

2321   waltzes and polkas by johann strauss: rosen aus dem süden; tritsch-tratsch; g'schichten aus dem wienerwald; champagne polka; wiener blut; schatzwalzer; wein weib und gesang; perpetuum mobile
recorded in april 1963 in the konzerthaus vienna
orchester der wiener staatsoper
carl schuricht, conductor
further issues: 5211-5212 (g'schichten), 6275 in set 6270-6279 (g'schichten), in a multiple commemorative lp set for carl schuricht, vanguard SRV 256 and columbia (japan) OW 7880
cd: denon (japan) 30CO 1341 and scribendum SC 011 (rosen, champagne,

wiener blut, wein weib und gesang and perpetuum mobile)

further selections from the recording also on 7028

2322   dvorak cello concerto and two legends for orchestra
recorded in the konzerhaus vienna
orchester der wiener staatsoper
hans swarowsky, conductor
bernard greenhouse, cello
further issue: in 6-lp set but retaining same catalogue number

2323   dvorak piano trio in e minor op 90 & mendelssohn piano trio no 1 in d minor op 49
beaux arts trio
further issue: 3079 (dvorak)

2324   stravinsky le sacre du printemps and four etudes
recorded in 1963 in the maison de la radio paris
orchestre national
pierre boulez, conductor
further issues: in a 12-lp set of ballet music but retaining same catalogue number, nonesuch HB 71093 and festival classique FC 430
cd: ades 13 2222

2326   mozart symphonies nos 38 k504 and 41 k551
recorded in june 1963 in paris
orchestre du theatre national de l'opera
carl schuricht, conductor
further issue: in 6-lp set but retaining same catalogue number
cd: denon (japan) 30CO 1335 (no 41), 30CO 1336 (no 38) and scribendum SC 011

2327   **works for piano and orchestra**   see 198 and 2190

2332   **beethoven symphonies nos 2 in d & 4 in b flat**
recorded in october 1963 in the musikhalle hamburg
sinfonieorchester des norddeutschen rundfunks
pierre monteux, conductor
further issue: in 7-lp set of beethoven symphonies but retaining
same catalogue number
cd: emi CZS 575 4752 (no 2 only), fnac musique 642 302
and scribendum SC 013

2333   **tchaikovsky symphony no 5 in e minor op 64**
recorded in october 1963 in the musikhalle hamburg
sinfonieorchester des norrdeutschen rundfunks
pierre monteux, conductor
further issues: 6207 in set 6201-6212 and in 6-lp set retaining
same catalogue number
cd: priceless D 14155 and scribendum SC 013

2335   see 68
2336   see 2312

2337   **chopin the fourteen valses**
vlado perlemuter, piano
further issue: in 6-lp set but retaining same catalogue number
selections from the recording also on 507, 913, 941, 959, 5213-5214,
6212 and 7024

2341   see 208 and 2313

2345   **lehar die lustige witwe, sung in english**
broadway light opera society
boris mersson, conductor
edith lang and norma schinabeck, sopranos
john malony, tenor
robert bennett, baritone

2346   **lehar die lustige witwe, sung in french**
orchestre et choeurs des concerts de paris
boris mersson, conductor
lina dachary and olga milea, sopranos
pierre mollet, tenor
aime doniat, baritone

2347   **lehar die lustige witwe**
wiener operettenensemble
boris mersson, conductor
ruth rohner and hanneke van bork, sopranos
franz lindauer, tenor
fritz peter, baritone
excerpts from the recording also on M 566

2348   **lehar das land des lächelns**
hamburger operettenensemble
boris mersson, conductor
edith lang and olga milea, sopranos
pierre mollet, tenor
aime doniat, baritone

2349   **lehar das land des lächelns, sung in french**

orchestre et choeurs des concerts de paris
lina dachary and olga milea, sopranos
pierre mollet, tenor
aime doniat, baritone

2350   **lehar das land des lächelns, sung in english**
broadway light opera society
boris mersson, conductor
edith lang and norma schinabeck, sopranos
john malony, tenor
robert bennett, baritone

2353   see 2227

2356   **immortal melodies for cello and orchestra: works by bach, dvorak, tchaikovsky, mozart, rimsky-korsakov, albeniz, saint-saens, brahms, handel, martini, chopin and verdi**
orchestre des concerts de paris
jean-marie auberson, conductor
pierre fournier, cello
further issue: 2369
selections from the recording also on 513, 2785, 5223-5224 and 7020

2357   berlioz symphonie fantastique
recorded between 6-14 february 1964 in the musikhalle hamburg
sinfonieorchester des norddeutschen rundfunks
pierre monteux, conductor
further issues: 5213 and festival classique FC 404
cd: scribendum SC 013

2358   handel four organ concerti from op 4
geneva baroque orchestra
jean-marie auberson, conductor
lionel rogg, organ

2359   mozart symphonies nos 35 k385 and 39 k543
recorded between 6-14 february 1964 in the musikhalle hamburg
sinfonieorchester des norddeutschen rundfunks
pierre monteux, conductor
further issues: 5034 (no 35) and turnabout TV 34831
cd: scribendum SC 013

2360   oboe concerti by j.s. & c.p.e.bach, marcello and bellini
geneva baroque orchestra
jean-marie auberson, conductor
heinz holliger, oboe
lorand fenyves, violin
further issue: 5215-5216 (marcello and bellini)

**2361   tchaikovsky romeo and juliet, mussorgsky night on
bare mountain and rimsky-korsakov capriccio espagnol**
recorded between 6-14 february 1964 in the musikhalle hamburg
sinfonieorchester des norddeutschen rundfunks
pierre monteux, conductor
further issues: 528 (rimsky), 2548 (mussorgsky), 3048 (tchaikovsky),
3057 (tchaikovsky), turnabout TV 34668 and vanguard SRV 257
cd: scribendum SC 013

**2362   wagner der fliegende holländer overture, tristan und
isolde prelude and liebestod and tannhäuser overture and
venusberg music**
recorded between 6-14 february 1964 in the musikhalle hamburg
sinfonieorchester des norddeutschen rundfunks
pierre monteux, conductor
further issues: 2684 (holländer), 6277 in set 6270-6279 (tristan)
and festival classique FC 435
cd: scribendum SC 013

2363   abraham blume von hawai and jessel schwarzwaldmädel, scenes from the operettas
hamburger operettenensemble
eddy mers, conductor
sonja michael and nancy mckay, sopranos
rolf sommerfeld, tenor

2364   beethoven piano sonatas nos 8, 20 and 23
friedrich gulda, piano
further issues: 2916, 6236 (nos 8 and 23) and 6240 (no 20)
cd: scribendum SC 016 (nos 8 and 23)
6236 and 6240 were part of a multiple lp set containing the complete piano sonatas

2365   schubert impromptus d899 & 6 moments musicaux
friedrich gulda, piano
further issue: in 6-lp set but retaining same catalogue number
cd: scribendum SC 016

2369   see 2356

2370   the virtuoso harpsichord: pieces by byrd, farnaby, purcell, rameau, handel, scarlatti, soler, albeniz & couperin
fernando valente, harpsichord

2371 (2-lp)   verdi rigoletto
recorded in 1964 in the konzerthaus vienna
orchester und chor der wiener staatsoper
gianfranco rivoli, conductor
anna machianti, soprano
nedda casei, contralto
michele molese, tenor
licino montefusco, baritone
federico davia, bass
further issues: in 6-lp set of verdi operas and festival classique CFC 60013
excerpts from the recording also on 2384

2374   see 2282

2376 (2-lp)   mozart mass in c minor k427
recorded in the konzerthaus vienna
orchester und chor der wiener staatsoper
jean-marie auberson, conductor
maria stader, soprano
nedda casei, contralto
waldemar kmentt, tenor
heinz rehfuss, baritone
further issue: in 6-lp set of mozart choral music but retaining same
catalogue number

2377   **recital of organ music by bach**
recorded in 1964 in the grossmünster zürich
andre marchal, organ

2378 (2-lp)   bach the six brandenburg concerti

recorded in may 1966 in zürich
zürich baroque ensemble
carl schuricht, conductor
further issues: 547 (no 2), 955 (no 3), 2684 (no 2), 6201 in set
6201-6212 (no 3), in 6-lp set retaining same catalogue number,
in a multiple commemorative lp set for carl schuricht and
columbia (japan) OW 7876-7877
cd: denon (japan) 30CO 1343-1344, scribendum SC 011 and
preludio PHC 1120-1121
assistant conductor for these recordings was boris mersson

2379   **handel the water music**
recorded in 1964 in the kurhaus den haag
residentieorkest
pierre boulez, conductor
further issues: nonesuch HB 71127 and festival classique FC 413
cd: ades 13 2342 and CD 104
excerpts from the recording also on 2548 and 2784

2380   **music for christmas by bach and corelli**
see 190 and 2057

2381   **works by grieg**
piano concerto in a minor
recorded in the konzerhaus vienna
wiener symphoniker
jean-marie auberson, conductor
menaham pressler, piano
orchestra described on this recording as vienna festival orchestra
holberg suite
ramat gan chamber orchestra
eliahu inbal, conductor

2382   **lieder by mozart, schubert, schumann and wolf**
recorded in 1965 in the konzerthaus vienna
irmgard seefried, soprano
walter klien, piano
further issue: pearl SHE 556-557

2383   vienna city of dreams: waltzes and polkas by johann and josef strauss, lanner, komzak and waldteufel
recorded in the konzerthaus vienna
orchester der wiener staatsoper
anton paulik, conductor
further issues: 2685 (strauss), 5213-5214 (lanner) and 6275 in set
6270-6279 (lanner)

2384   see 2371

2394   bruckner symphony no 7 in e
recorded in september 1964 in the kurhaus den haag
residentieorkest
carl schuricht, conductor
further issues: nonesuch HB 71139 and columbia (japan) OC 7259
cd: denon (japan) 30CO 1339, preludio PHC 1126 and scribendum SC 011

2395   brahms piano concerto no 2 in b flat op 83
recorded on 27-28 september 1964 in the kurhaus den haag
residentieorkest
willem van otterloo, conductor
nikita magaloff, piano
further issue: in 6-lp set but retaining original catalogue number
cd: preludio PHC 1125 and ages 509 0102

2399   bach magnificat and cantata no 57
recorded in the konzerthaus vienna
orchester und chor der wiener staatsoper
jean-marie auberson, conductor
maria stader, soprano
nedda casei, contralto
waldemar kmentt, tenor
federico davia and heinz rehfuss, baritones

2400 (2-lp)   beethoven symphonies nos 8 and 9 "choral"
recorded between 17-19 september 1964 in the kurhaus den haag
residentieorkest
toonkunstkoor amsterdam
willem van otterloo, conductor
maria stader, soprano
sophia van sante, contralto
eric tappy, tenor
franz crass, bass
further issues: 2717 (no 9), 2813 (no 9), 3072-3073 and in a 7-lp set of
beethoven symphonies but retaining original catalogue number

2406   tchaikovsky piano concerto no 1 in b flat and chopin krakowiak for piano and orchestra
recorded in march 1964 (tchaikovsky) and on 26 september 1964 (chopin) in the kurhaus den haag
residentieorkest
willem van otterloo, conductor
nikita magaloff, piano
further issues: 2920 (chopin), 3045 (tchaikovsky), 3049 (tchaikvsky), 6208 in set 6201-6212 (tchaikovsky) and in 6-lp set but retaining original catalogue number
cd: ages 509 0052 (tchaikovsky) and 509 0102 (chopin)

2407   haydn symphonies nos 94 "surprise" and 100 "military"
recorded in the konzerthaus vienna
orchester der wiener staatsoper
david josefowitz, conductor
further issue: in 6-lp set but retaining same catalogue number

2408   chopin piano concerto no 1 & andante spianato
recorded in the konzerhaus vienna
orchester der wiener staatsoper
david josefowitz, conductor (concerto)
jean-marie auberson, conductor (andante spianato)
menahem pressler, piano
further issue: in 6-lp set but retaining same catalogue number

2409   see 2184

2410   works by max bruch
recorded in the konzerthaus vienna
violin concerto no 1 in g minor
orchester der wiener staatsoper
jean-marie auberson, conductor
tibor varga, violin
kol nidrei for cello and orchestra
orchester der wiener staatsoper
heinz wallberg, conductor
aurora natola, cello

2411   tchaikovsky violin concerto in d and meditation
recorded in the konzerthaus vienna
orchester der wiener staatsoper
boris mersson, conductor (concerto)
jean-marie auberson, conductor (meditation)
tibor varga, violin
further issues: 3046 (concerto) and in 6-lp set but retaining same catalogue number

2412   **grieg symphonic dances and lyric suite**
recorded in the konzerthaus vienna
orchester der wiener staatsoper
gianfranco rivoli, conductor
further issue: 521 (lyric suite)

2413   see 2286

2415   **operatic arias by verdi**
excerpts from previously published recordings

2416 (2-lp)   verdi il trovatore
recorded in 1965 in the konzerthaus vienna
orchester und chor der wiener staatsoper
nello santi, conductor
virginia gordoni, soprano
nedda casei, contralto
michele molese, tenor
lino puglisi, baritone
tugomir franc, bass
further issue: in 6-lp set of verdi operas
excerpts from the recording also on 2461 and 7025

2417   **schubert string quartet d804 and quartettsatz d87**
quartetto italiano
cd: ages 509 0032

2418   **haydn string quartets op 33 no 2 and op 76 no 3**
quartetto italiano
further issue: in 6-lp set but retaining same catalogue number
cd: ages 509 0032

2419   see CHC 44
2420   see CHS 1231

2422 (2-lp)   beethoven missa solemnis in d op 123
recorded in the konzerthaus vienna
orchester und chor der wiener staatsoper
heinz wallberg, conductor
teresa stich-randall, soprano
nedda casei, contralto
murray dickie, tenor
frederick guthrie, bass

2423 **splendours of the middle ages and renaissance**
capella instrumentalis geneva
blaise pidaux and pierre pernoud, conductors

2426 **schuetz historia der geburt jesu**
recorded in the konzerthaus vienna
orchester der wiener staatsoper
hans swarowsky, conductor
teresa stich-randall, soprano
kurt equiluz, tenor
nikolaus simkowsky, bass

2433 **vocal works by stravinsky: les noces; berceuses du chat; pribaoutki; four russian songs; four peasant songs**
recorded in 1965 in paris
instrumentalistes et choeurs du theatre national de l'opera
pierre boulez, conductor
jacqueline brumaire, soprano
denise scharley, mezzo-soprano
further issue: nonesuch HB 71133
cd: ades 13 2362

2435 **mozart divertimenti k136, k137 and k138 & adagio and fugue in c minor k546**
ramat gan chamber orchestra
eliahu inbal, conductor
further issue: 6272 in set 6270-6279 (k136)

2439 **haydn mass in b flat "theresienmesse"**
recorded in the konzerthaus vienna
orchester und chor der wiener staatsoper
hans swarowsky, conductor
annelies hückel, soprano
nedda casei, contralto
adolf dallapozza, tenor
nikolaus simowsky, bass
further issue: 6379 in set 6376-6383

2440 **schubert symphonies nos 2 d125 & 3 d200**
recorded in the konzerthaus vienna
orchester der wiener staatsoper
david josefowitz, conductor
further issue: 2462 (no 3)

2441   **overtures by berlioz, offenbach, cherubini, lortzing & weber**
recorded in the konzerthaus vienna
orchester der wiener staatsoper
hans swarowsky, conductor
further issue: 2734 (berlioz and offenbach)

2442   **works by bruckner and mahler**
recorded in may 1965 in the konzerthaus vienna
orchester der wiener staatsoper
heinz wallberg, conductor
te deum
wiener jeunesse choir
teresa stich-randall, soprano
sonja draksler, contralto
murray dickie, tenor
frederick guthrie, bass
further issue: 2604
kindertotenlieder
hilde rössel-majdan, contralto
further issue: 2800-2801

2444   **recital of piano music by chopin**
nikita magaloff, piano
further issue: in 6-lp set but retaining same catalogue number

2445   **dvorak symphony no 8 in g op 88 and carnival**
overture op 92/mercury recording
recorded on 19-20 june 1959 in the town hall watford
london symphony orchestra
antal dorati, conductor
mercury issues: MG 50236, MG 50323 (overture), SR 90236,
SR 90323 (overture), SR 90516 (overture), MGW 14080,
SRW 18080, MMA 11128 and AMS 16075
cd: philips mercury 434 3122 (symphony)

2446   **strauss don juan & tod und verklärung/**mercury recording
recorded on 23 december 1958 in the winthrop auditorium minneapolis

minneapolis symphony orchestra
antal dorati, conductor
mercury issues: MG 50202, MG 50334, SR 90202, SR 90334,
SRI 75015 (don juan), MMA 11125 and AMS 16075
other lp issues: philips classical favourites GL 5831, SGL 5831,
642 270GL and 837 879GY
cd: philips mercury 434 3482

2447   recital of organ works by bach
recorded in 1966 in the grossmünster zürich
andre marchal, organ

2448   unsterbliche operette: scenes from paganini, viktoria und ihr husar, maske in blau and madame pompadour
zürcher operettenensemble
boris mersson, conductor

2449   see 2200

2450 (2-lp)   honegger le roi david

orchestre du theatre national de l'opera
chorale elisabeth brasseur
serge baudo, conductor
jacqueline brumaire, soprano
denise scharley, mezzo-soprano
jacques pottier, baritone

2457   telemann wassermusik, trumpet concerto & les nations

paris baroque orchestra
david josefowitz, conductor

2459   see 2115 and 2116

2460   ewig junge operette: scenes from der vetter aus dingsda, der graf von luxemburg and die dollarprinzessin
zürcher operettenensemble
boris mersson, conductor
wiener operettenensemble
david josefowitz, conductor

2461   see 2416
2462   see 2139 and 2440

2465   mendelssohn symphony no 3 "scotch" and hebrides overture/mercury recording
recorded on 5-6 july 1956 in the town hall walthamstow
london symphony orchestra
antal dorati, conductor
mercury issues: MG 50123, MG 50323 (overture), SR 90123,
SR 90323 (overture), MGW 14056, SRW 18056 and MMA 11048
other lp issue: philips SDL 502
cd: decca collection classique 464 3632 (overture) and
philips mercury 434 3632

2466   brahms piano quartet op 34
members of the warsaw string quartet
wladyslav szpilman, piano

**2467   england's golden age: works by byrd, morley,
parsons, dowland, wilbye, weelkes and tallis**
the deller consort

**2468   french organ masters: works by marchand,
grigny, couperin, clerembault and guilan**
francis chapelet, organ

2469   bloch concerto grosso & schoenberg verklärte nacht
jerusalem chamber orchestra
mendi roden, conductor
frank pelleg, piano

**2470   bach concerti for two, three and four harpsichords
bwv 1060, bwv 1064 and bwv 1065**
jerusalem chamber orchestra
mendi roden, conductor
frank pelleg, christiane jacottet, lieselotte born and
andre löv, harpsichords
further issues: 5205-5206 (bwv1065) and in 6-lp set retaining
same catalogue number

2471   harpsichord concerti by the bach family
jerusalem chamber orchestra
mendi roden, conductor
frank pelleg, harpsichord
further issue: 5205-5206 (w.f.bach)

**2476   charme de l'operette: scenes from works by lehar,
kalman and messager**
boris mersson and andre gallois, conductors

2477   songs of the british isles
linden players and singers
ian humphries, conductor

2478   symphonies by romantic composers
mendelssohn symphony no 5 in d/mercury recording
recorded on 21 march 1958 in the paradise theatre detroit
detroit symphony orchestra
paul paray, conductor
mercury issues: MG 50174, SR 90174, MGW 14067,
SRW 18067, MMA 11032 and AMS 16022
cd: philips mercury 434 3962
schumann symphony no 4 in d minor
recorded on 28 september 1964 in the kurhaus den haag
residentieorkest
willem van otterloo, conductor
further issues: 3076 and 5207-5208

2481 (3-lp)   puccini madama butterfly

recorded in 1966 in the konzerthaus vienna
orchester und chor der wiener staatsoper
nello santi, conductor
virginia gordoni, soprano
nedda casei, contralto
michele molese, tenor
valerio meucci, baritone
further issue: in 6-lp set of puccini operas
excerpts from the recording also on 2497

**2482   famous marches by mozart, beethoven, mendelsssohn,
johann strauss, meyerbeer, berlioz and wagner**
recorded in the konzerthaus vienna
orchester der wiener staatsoper
hans swarowsky, conductor

2483   haydn nelson mass

recorded in the konzerthaus vienna
orchester und chor der wiener staatsoper
hans swarowsky, conductor
teresa stich-randall, soprano
nedda casei, contralto
kurt equiluz, tenor
nikolaus simkowsky, bass
further issues: 6378 in set 6376-6383 and nonesuch HB 71173

2484   mozart clarinet concerto k622 & horn conceri k412 & k447
recorded in the konzerhaus vienna
orchester der wiener staatsoper
wilfried böttcher, conductor
rolf eichler, clarinet
robert freund, horn
further issue: 5216-5217 (k412)

2485   **haydn symphonies nos 96 "miracle" and 102**
recorded in the konzerthaus vienna
orchester der wiener staatsoper
david josefowitz, conductor

2486   **telemann machet die tore weit, cantata;**
bach cantata no 131 "süsser trost mein jesus kommt"
recorded in the konzerthaus vienna
wiener barockorchester
wiener kammerchor
wilfried böttcher, conductor
teresa stich-randall, soprano
nedda casei, contralto
kurt equiluz, tenor
ernst gerold schramm, bass

2487   **mozart piano concerti nos 17 k453 and 24 k491**

recorded in the konzerthaus vienna
wiener kammerorchester
wilfried böttcher, conductor
menahem pressler, piano

2488   **liszt piano concerti nos 1 and 2**
zürich radio orchestra
serge baudo, conductor
nikita magaloff, piano
further issues: 6210 in set 6201-6212 (concerto no 1) and
festival classique FC 417

2489   **bruckner symphony no 4 in e flat   "romantic"**
recorded in 1967 in the konzerthaus vienna
orchester der wiener staatsoper
heinz wallberg, conductor

2490   **ravel valses nobles et sentimentales, alborada del**
gracioso, bolero and pavane pour une infante defunte
recorded in the maison de la radio paris
orchestre national
maurice le roux, conductor
further issues: 5213-5214 (valses), 6279 in set 6270-6279 (bolero
and pavane) and festival classique FC 425

2491   chamber works by bartok
sonata for two pianos and percussion
genevieve joy and jacqueline robin, pianos
jean-claude casadesus and jean-pierre drouet, percussion
contrasts for violin, clarinet and piano
lorand fenyves, violin
robert gugolz, clarinet
livia rev, piano

2494   debussy iberia; albeniz iberia
recorded between october-december 1966 in the maison de la radio paris

orchestre national
charles munch, conductor
further issues: 2761 (debussy), festival classique FC 437 and
nonesuch HB 71189
cd: scribendum SC 012

2495   bizet: symphony in c; jeux d'enfants; patrie overture
recorded on 10-11 november 1966 in the maison de la radio paris
orchestre national
charles munch, conductor
further issue: 528 (patrie), 5207-5208 (symphony) and
nonesuch HB 71183
cd: emi CZS 575 4772 (symphony), ades 13 2242 and
scribendum SC 012

2496   works by couperin, forqueray, telemann & marcello
marcal cervera, viola da gamba
christiane jacottet, harpsichord

2497   see 2481

2510   string quartets by ravel and debussy
quatuor de geneve

2511   festival of russian music: rimsky-korsakov russian
easter festival overure & introduction et cortege from le coq d'or;
borodin in the steppes of central asia; mussorgsky khovantschina
recorded in october-november 1966 in the maison de la radio paris
orchestre national
charles munch, conductor
further issues: 5211-5212 (borodin) and festival classique FC 439
cd: fnac musique 642 330 (rimsky-korsakov) and scribendum SC 012

2512   franck violin sonata & dvorak sonatina for violin and piano

denes zsigmondi, violin
annelise nissen-zsigmondi, piano

2513   chamber music by franck and debussy
franck piano quintet
warsaw string quartet
wladyslaw szpilman, piano
debussy cello sonata
aldo parisot, cello
lester taylor, piano

2514-2517 (4-lp)   handel complete organ concerti op 4
collegium academicum geneva
robert dunand, conductor
lionel rogg, organ
further issues: 2528 (nos 9, 10, 11 and 12), 2529 (nos 13, 14, 15 and 16),
5205-5206 (no 15), 5209-5210 (no 13) and 6201 in set 6201-6212 (no 4)

2518 (2-lp)   monteverdi vespro della beata vergine
recorded in 1968 in the maison de la radio paris
orchestre national et choeurs
deller consort
maurice le roux, conductor

2519   franck symphony in d minor
recorded between september-november 1966 in de doelen rotterdam
rotterdam philharmonic orchestra
charles munch, conductor
further issue: festival classique FC 411
cd: accord 22 0272 and scribendum SC 012

2526   works by bach, beethoven, mayer, rosetti & krumpholz
nicanor zabaleta, harp

2527   beethoven symphony no 6 in f op 68 "pastoral"
recorded in september 1966 in de doelen rotterdam
rotterdam philharmonic orchestra
charles munch, conductor
further issue: in 7-lp set of complete beethoven symphonies but
retaining same catalogue number
cd: valois V 4829 and scribendum SC 012

2528-2529   see 2516-2517

2530   brahms clarinet quintet/everest recording
fine arts string quartet
reginald kell, clarinet

2531   bach goldberg variations
christiane jacottet, harpsichord

2532   respighi i pini di roma & fontane di roma/everest recording
recorded between 21-24 october 1959 in the town hall walthamstow
london symphony orchestra
sir malcolm sargent, conductor
everest issues: LPBR 6051 and SDBR 3051
further issues: world records CM 27 and SCM 27 and
hallmark HM 502 and SHM 502

2533   orchestral works by russian composers/everest recording
leopold stokowski, conductor
prokofiev cinderella, suite from the ballet
recorded on 8 october 1958 in new york
new york philharmonic
everest issues: LPBR 6016, LPBR 6108, SDBR 3016 and SDBR 3108
other issues: 6441 in set 6436-6441 and world records T 173 and ST 173
cd: everest EVC 9023, bescol CD 519 and priceless D 2269
orchestra described on this recording as stadium symphony orchestra

scriabin poeme de l'extase
recorded on 19 march 1958 in houston
houston symphony orchestra
everest issues: LPBR 6032 and SDBR 3032
cd: everest EVC 9037, philips 422 3062 and pantheon D 1032X

2534   khachaturian piano concerto/everest recording
recorded on 10 november 1959 in the town hall walthamstow
london symphony orchestra
hugo rignold, conductor
peter katin, piano
everest issues: LPBR 6055 and SDBR 3055
other issues: world records CM 55 and SCM 55 and
hallmark HM 530 and SHM 530
cd: everest EVC 9060

2535   beethoven string quartets op 18 nos 3 & 4
fine arts string quartet
everest issue: SDBR 3255
further issue: 6222 in set 6221-6226
originally published on the fine arts quartet's own label (concertapes)

2536   de falla the three-cornered hat, ballet/everest recording
recorded on 23-24 november 1959 in the town hall walthamstow
london symphony orchestra
enrique jorda, conductor
barbara howitt, mezzo-soprano
everest issues: LPBR 6057 and SDBR 3057
other issues: world records T 164 and ST 164 and
hallmark HM 540 and SHM 540
cd: everest EVC 9000
excerpts from the recording also on 5219-5220

2537   tchaikovsky swan lake, scenes from the ballet
recorded in the konzerthaus vienna
orchester der wiener staatsoper
nello santi, conductor
further issue: in 12-lp set of ballet music but retaining same
catalogue number
excerpts from the recording also on 5203-5204 and 6439 in set 6436-6441

2538   prokofiev symphony no 5 in b flat/everest recording
recorded between 18-20 may 1959 in the town hall walthamstow
london symphony orchestra
sir malcolm sargent, conductor
everest issues: LPBR 6034 and SDBR 3034
other issues: world records CM 29 and SCM 29 and
hallmark HM 537 and SHM 537
cd: everest EVC 9043

2539   chopin mazurkas and polonaises, selection

menahem pressler, piano

further issue: in 6-lp set but retaining same catalogue number

2540   beethoven egmont, complete incidental music
recorded in the konzerthaus vienna
orchester der wiener staatsoper
heinz wallberg, conductor
wendy fine, soprano
karl eidlitz, narrator
further issue: in 6-lp set of beethoven stage works

2541   bruckner symphony no 9 in d minor
recorded in 1968 in the konzerthaus vienna
orchester der wiener staatsoper
heinz wallberg, conductor

2542 (4-lp)   bach matthäus-passion
recorded in the konzerthaus vienna
orchester der wiener staatsoper
wiener akademiechor and sängerknaben
hans swarowsky, conductor
heather harper, soprano
gertrude jahn, contralto
kurt equiluz, tenor
marius rintzler, baritone
jakob stämpfli, bass
further issue: in 6-lp set of bach choral music but
retaining same catalgue number
excerpts from the recording also on 2764; orchestra described on this
recording as wiener symphoniker

2544   corelli four sonatas for violin and continuo
devy erlih, violin
liselotte born, harpsichord
francois courvoisier, cello

2545   haydn mass no 4 "nicolaimesse"
recorded in the konzerthaus vienna
orchester der wiener staatsoper
wiener akademiechor
georg barati, conductor
elisabeth thomann, soprano
rose bahl, contralto
kurt equiluz, tenor
gerhard eder, bass

2550   beethoven christus am ölberge, oratorio
recorded in the konzerthaus vienna
orchester und chor der wiener staatsoper
david josefowitz, conductor
wendy fine, soprano
kurt equiluz, tenor
marius rintzler, baritone

2551   brahms double concerto & schubert rondo d483
recorded in the konzerthaus vienna
orchester der wiener staatsoper
moshe atzmon, conductor
igor ozim, violin
siegfried palm, cello
further issue: 3075

2552   bach violin concerti nos 1 and 2
recorded in the konzerthaus vienna
wiener barockorchester
moshe atzmon, conductor
wolfgang schneiderhan, violin
further issue: in 6-lp set but retaining same catalogue number

2553   beethoven piano concerto no 1 and rondo in b flat
recorded in the konzerthaus vienna
orchester der wiener staatsoper
moshe atzmon, conductor
menahem pressler, piano
further issue: in 6-lp set of beethoven concerti but retaining
same catalogue number

2554   brahms serenade no 1 in d op 11
recorded in the konzerthaus vienna
orchester der wiener staatsoper
moshe atzmon, conductor

2555   organ works by frescobaldi, gabrieli, santa maria, cabecon, cabanilles, muffat, pachelbel and fischer
herbert tachezi, organ

2556   beethoven piano concerti nos 2 in b flat & 4 in g
zürich radio orchestra
gianfranco rivoli, conductor
nikita magaloff, piano
further issues: 5205-5206 (no 2) and in 6-lp set of beethoven
concerti but retaining same catalogue number

2557   ballet music by rossini, donizetti and verdi
zürich radio orchestra
gianfranco rivoli, conductor
further issue: in 12-lp set of ballet music but retaining same
catolgue number
selection from the recording also on 6436 in set 6436-6441

2559   sibelius violin concerto & tapiola/everest recording
recorded between 5-7 november 1959 in the town hall walhamstow
london symphony orchestra
tauno hannikainen, conductor
tossy spivakovsky, violin
everest issues: LPBR 6045 and SDBR 3045
further issues: world records T 94 and ST 94
cd: everest EVC 9025 (concerto) and EVC 9035 (tapiola)

2560   see 2167

2562   mozart serenade no 7 "haffner"/supraphon recording
prague chamber orchestra
josef suk, conductor and violin
cd: supraphon 3617 2011

2567   bruckner symphony no 3 in d minor
radio-sinfonie-orchester berlin
lorin maazel, conductor
further issue: festival classique FC 405

2570   tchaikovsky sleeping beauty, scenes from the ballet
radio-sinfonie-orchester berlin
lorin maazel, conductor
further issues: in 6-lp and 12-lp sets retaining same catalogue number

and festival classique FC 433

excerpts from the recording also on 584, 5201-5202 and 6440 in set 6436-6441

2574   brahms piano quartet op 26
members of the brahms string quartet
pier narciso masi, piano

2577   landowski les adieux
orchestra and chorus of radio luxembourg
louis de froment, conductor

2578   recital of piano music by debussy
nikita magaloff, piano

2579   debussy la mer and trois nocturnes
recorded in february 1968 in the maison de la radio paris
orchestre national
charles munch, conductor
further issues: 5209-5210 (la mer), 6279 in set 6270-6279 (la mer)
and festival classique FC 408
cd: scribendum SC 012 (la mer) and accord 22 0272

2580   masterpieces of the baroque: works by monteverdi, strizzio, de wert, gesualdo and gasteldi
accademia monteverdiana
denis stevens, conductor

2581   **kalman gräfin maritza**
orchester und chor der wiener volksoper
franz bauer-theussel, conductor
lotte rysanek, soprano
else liebesberg, mezzo-soprano
rudolf christ, tenor
herbert prikopa, bass

2583   see 146, 203, 2076 and 2119

2585 (3-lp)   bach weihnachtsoratorium
recorded in the konzerthaus vienna
orchester der wiener staatsoper
wiener kammerchor
hans swarowsky, conductor
heather harper, soprano
ruth hesse, contralto
kurt equiluz and thomas page, tenors
kieth engen, bass
further issue: in 6-lp set of bach choral works but retaining
same catalogue number
excerpts from the recording also on 2763

2586   **mozart le nozze di figaro, scenes from the opera**
recorded in 1968 in the konzerthaus vienna
orchester der wiener staatsoper
heinz wallberg, conductor
heather harper and oliviera miljakovic, sopranos
rohangiz yachmi, mezzo-soprano
heinz holecek and rudolf jedlicka, baritone

2587   see 2410

2590   **berio sequenza IV; boulez sonatas 1 and 3;
webern klavierstück op posth. and variations op 27**
claude helffer, piano

2591   **oscar straus ein walzertraum and schroder
hochzeitsnacht in paradies, scenes from the operettas**
recorded in the konzerthaus vienna
orchester und solisten der wiener staatsoper
franz bauer-theussel, conductor

2593   **mozart requiem in d minor k626**
recorded in 1968 in the konzerthaus vienna
orchester der wiener staatsoper
wiener kammerchor
pierre colombo, conductor
heather harper, soprano
ruth hesse, contralto
thomas page, tenor
kieth engen, bass
further issues: in 6-lp set of mozart choral music but retaining
same catalogue number and festival classique FC 421

2594   **beethoven triple concerto in c op 56**
recorded in 1968 in the konzerthaus vienna
orchester der wiener staatsoper
heinz wallberg, conductor
claude helffer, piano
igor ozim, violin
aurora natola, cello
further issue: in 6-lp set of beethoven concerti but retaining
same catalogue number

2595   **johann strauss frühlingsstimmen; frisch ins feld;
lagunenwalzer; neue pizzicato polka; seid umschlungen;
vergnügungszug; wo die zitronen blüh'n**
recorded in 1968 in the konzerthaus vienna
orchester der wiener staatsoper
heinz wallberg, conductor

2596   **bach selection from the wohltemperiertes klavier**
christiane jaccottet, harpsichord

2597   **schubert symphony no 9 in c d944 "great"**
recorded in 1969 in the konzerthaus vienna
orchester der wiener staatsoper
david josefowitz, conductor

2598   **wagner parsifal prelude, siegfried waldweben,
walkürenritt & götterdämmerung rheinfahrt & trauermarsch**
recorded in the konzerthaus vienna
orchester der wiener staatsoper
heinz wallberg, conductor
further issue: 5209-5210 (waldweben)

2599   **clarinet quintets by mozart and weber**
quatuor de geneve
robert gugolz, clarinet

2600   recital of lieder by schubert
recorded in 1968 in the konzerthaus vienna
irmgard seefried, soprano
erik werba, piano
further issues: in 6-lp set but retaining same catalogue number,
festival classique FC 483 and pearl SHE 556-557
cd: ades 13 2272

2601   couperin pieces de clavecin
christiane jaccottet, harpsichord
marcal cervera, viola da gamba

2602   bartok concerto for orchestra/everest recording
recorded on 30-31 march 1960 in houston
houston symphony orchestra
leopold stokowski, conductor
everest issues: LPBR 6069 and SDBR 3069
further issues: world records CM 36 and SCM 36, hallmark HM 590
and SHM 590 and dell arte DA 9013
cd: everest EVC 9008

2603   arriaga string quartets nos 1 and 2
quatuor de geneve

2604 (2-lp)   works by bruckner
symphony no 8 in c minor
recorded in 1968 in the konzerthaus vienna
orchester der wiener staatsoper
heinz wallberg, conductor
te deum   see 2442

2605   potpourri franz lehar
orchester der wiener staatsoper
boris mersson, conductor

2612 (2-lp)   berlioz l'enfance du christ
recorded in the maison de la radio paris
orchestre national et choeurs
jean martinon, conductor
jane berbie, mezzo-soprano
alain vanzo, tenor
roger soyer and claude cales, baritones

2615   haydn symphonies nos 92 and 103
radio-sinfonie-orchester berlin
lorin maazel, conductor
further issues: in 6-lp set but retaining same catalogue number
and festival classique FC 414

2623   bach selections from orgelbüchlein & klavierübung
herbert tachezi, organ

2625   couperin trois concerts royaux
hans-heinz schneeberger, violin
claude viala, cello
brigitte buxtorf, flute
christiane jaccottet, harpsichord

2626   mozart symphonies nos 25 k183 and 29 k201
radio-sinfonie-orchester berlin
lorin maazel, conductor

2631   dvorak serenade for strings & czech suite/supraphon
prague chamber orchestra
further issue: in 6-lp set but retaining same catalogue number

2633   recital of piano music by chopin
arthur moreira lima, piano

2638   mahler symphony no 4 in g
radio-sinfonie-orchester berlin
lorin maazel, conductor
heather harper, soprano
further issues: festival classique FC 418, nonesuch HB 71259
and pearl SHE 552

2639   schubert string quintet in c d956
quatuor de geneve
janos scholz, cello

**2646   tchaikovsky romeo and juliet, marche slave and
capriccio italien**
recorded in 1969 in the salle garnier monte carlo
orchestre national de monte carlo
igor markevitch, conductor
further issue: 6274 in set 6270-6279
cd: ages 509 0012 (romeo and juliet)

**2647   bizet l'arlesienne, first and second suites from
the incidental music**
recorded in 1969 in the salle garnier monte carlo
orchestre national de monte carlo
igor markevitch, conductor
further issues: 5211-5212 (suite no 1) and 6278 in set
6270-6279 (suite no 1)
cd: ages 509 0012

2648   liszt les preludes, orpheus, mazeppa & mephisto waltz
recorded between 2-4 june 1969 in the salle garnier monte carlo
orchestre national de monte carlo
paul paray, conductor
further issues: 5201-5202 (mazeppa), 5213-5214 (mephisto waltz), 6277
in set 6270-6279 and festival classique FC 416

2649   mozart violin concerti no 3 k216 and no 5 k219
lausanne chamber orchestra
armin jordan, conductor
franco gulli, violin
further issues: 6272 in set 6270-6279 and in 6-lp set retaining same
catalogue number

2650   scenes from operas by cimarosa and paer
collegium academicum geneva
robert dunand, conductor
besia retchitzka, soprano
fernando corena, bass

2651   schubert three sonatinas for violin and piano
sidney harth, violin
dorel handman, piano

2652   beethoven the three piano quartets op posth.
members of the quartetto di roma
ornella santoliquido, piano
further issue: in set 6227-6232

2653   mendelssohn string symphonies in c minor and in d
jerusalem chamber orchestra
mendi roden, conductor

2654   sinfonias by the sons of bach
jerusalem chamber orchestra
mendi roden, conductor

2655   mozart flute concerto no 1 & horn concerti k417 & k495
recorded in the konzerthaus vienna
orchester der wiener staatsoper
karl österreicher and boris mersson, conductors
helmut riessberger, flute
robert freund, horn

2656   **bach das musikalische opfer**
paul kuentz chamber orchestra
christian larde, flute
monique frasca-colombier, violin
pierre cyprien, harpsichord

2657   **mozart flute concerto no 2 & flute & harp concerto**
paul kuentz chamber orchestra
christian larde, flute
marie-claire jamet, harp
further issues: 5216-5217 (flute concerto), in 6-lp set retaining
same catalogue number and festival classique FC 422

2659   **love songs from four centuries**
accademia monteverdiana
denis stevens, conductor

2660   **bartok dance suite & miraculous mandarin suite**
recorded in november 1969 in the salle garnier monte carlo
orchestre national de monte carlo
bruno maderna, conductor
cd: ages 509 0092

2661   **bartok piano concerto no 3 and prokofiev piano
concerto no 3**
recorded in november 1969 in the salle garnier monte carlo
orchestre national de monte carlo
bruno maderna, conductor
claude helffer, piano
further issue: festival classique FC 438

2662   see 2120

2663   **french orchestral music: dukas l'apprenti sorcier;
ravel la valse; chabrier espana and suite pastorale**
recorded in october 1969 in the salle garnier monte carlo
orchestre national de monte carlo
paul paray, conductor
further issues: 5201-5202 (dukas), 5211-5212 (espana), 6278 in set
6270-6279 (dukas and espana) and festival classique FC 440

2664   **schumann symphony no 1 and genoveva overture**
orchestre national de monte carlo
david josefowitz, conductor
further issue: in 6-lp set but retaining same catalogue number

**2665   orchestral works by prokofiev: symphony no 1 "classical",
l'amour des trois oranges & lieutenant kije, ballet suites**
orchestre national de monte carlo
david josefowitz, conductor

2672   piano concerti by arensky and albeniz
felicja blumenthal, piano
arensky piano concerto
brno philharmonic orchestra
jiri wildhans, conductor
albeniz concerto fantastico
rai torino orchestra
alberto zedda, conductor

2673   eighteenth century piano concerti
alberto zedda, conductor
felicja blumenthal, piano
clementi piano concerto in c
prague chamber orchestra
paisiello piano concerto in f
rai torino orchestra

2674   viotti piano concerto in g minor
rai torino orchestra
alberto zedda, conductor
felicja blumenthal, piano

2675   lalo symphonie espagnole & namouna ballet suite
orchestre national de monte carlo
rene klopfenstein, conductor
christian ferras, violin
further issue: festival classique FC 415

2676 (3-lp)   vivaldi il cimento, the 12 concerti op 8
collegium academicum geneva
david josefowitz, conductor
igor ozim, violin
*the four concerti from this recording which comprise le 4 stagioni also issued on
2701; further selections from the recording also on 2945 and 5209-5210*

2677   the virtuoso trumpet: works by italian composers
collegium academicum geneva
robert dunand, conductor
michel cuvit and michel debonneville, trumpets

2678   schumann carnaval & etudes symphoniques

nikita magaloff. piano
further issue: in 6-lp set but retaining same catalogue number

2679   see 2039

2682   mendelssohn symphony no 4 "italian" and schubert
overture in the italian style d591 no 2, alfonso und estrella
overture d731 and overture in e minor d648
recorded in 1968 in tokyo
japan philharmonic orchestra
igor markevitch, conductor
further issues: 3067 (schubert), 5207-5209 (mendelssohn), in 6-lp set
but retaining same catalogue number and festival classique FC 419
cd: scribendum SC 014

2688 (3-lp)   rossini il barbiere di siviglia
recorded in 1970 in the salle garnier monte carlo
orchestre national et choeurs de monte carlo
gianfranco rivoli, conductor
christiane eda-pierre, soprano
luigi alva, tenor
marco stecchi, baritone
andrew foldi, bass
further issues: in 6-lp set of rossini operas but retaining same
catalgue number and festival classique CFC 60004
excerpts from the recording also on 2762

2694   immortal melodies from the baroque
collegium academicum geneva
robert dunand, conductor

2695 (2-lp)   beethoven die geschöpfe des prometheus, ballet op 43
recorded in the salle garnier monte carlo
orchestre national de monte carlo
pierre colombo, conductor
further issue: 2740-2741 and in 6-lp set of beethoven stage works
four overtures by beethoven   see 2274
*a later issue of this lp, using the same catalogue number, substituted beethoven
symphony no 1 (219) for three of the overtures*

**2696   brahms viola sonata no 2, schumann märchenbilder
and weber andante and rondo ungarese**
nobuko imai, viola
nerine barrett, piano
further issue: 3078 (schumann)

2701   see 2676

2702-2705 (4-lp)   beethoven complete violin sonatas
christian ferras, violin
pierre barbizet, piano
further issue: in 7-lp set but retaining same catalogue numbers
sonatas 5 and 9 also issued in a 6-lp set of beethoven chamber music

2706-2708 (3-lp)   beethoven complete cello sonatas and variations
alexander stein, cello
boris mersson, piano
further issue: in 7-lp set but retaining same catalogue numbers

2709   recital of solo piano pieces by beethoven
dorel handman, piano
further issue: in a 7-lp set but retaining same catalogue number

2710   stravinsky l'oiseau de feu, complete ballet
recorded in the maison de la radio paris
orchestre national
lorin maazel, conductor
further issues: in a 12-lp set of ballet music but retaining same
catalogue number and festival classique FC 431

2717   see 2400

2721   recital of piano music by mussorgsky and chopin
israela margalit, piano

2722   music by manuel de falla
recorded in the salle garnier monte carlo
orchestre national de monte carlo
david josefowitz, conductor
el amor brujo
carol smith, mezzo-soprano
noches en los jardines de espana
pierre barbizet, piano
further issue: 5209-5210 (noches)

**2723   music for two pianos by chopin, schubert, mozart,
schumann and brahms**
denise duport and muriel slatkine, pianos

2724   **rossini il signor bruschino**
recorded in 1970
collegium academicum geneva
robert dunand, conductor
evelyn brunner, soprano
della jones, mezzo-soprano
mario marchisio, tenor
gaston presset, bass
excerpts from the recording also on 2780 in set 2779-2781

2725   **recital of scottish and irish songs by beethoven**

accademia monteverdiana
denis stevens, conductor
further issue: 6245 in set 6244-6249

2726   see 2178 and 2243
2727   see 68
2729   see 2215
2735   see 2374

2737-2739 (3-lp)   beethoven complete string trios
basel string trio
further issue: 6247-6249 in multiple lp set

2740-2741   see 2695

2742   **mozart concerti for two and three pianos**
collegium academicum geneva
robert dunand, conductor
denise dupont, muriel slatkine and oswald russell, pianos
further issue: 5205-5206 (double concerto)

2744   **mussorgsky-ravel pictures at an exhibition;**
glinka russlan and lyudmila and ivan susanin overtures
recorded in the salle garnier monte carlo
orchestre national de monte carlo
david josefowitz, conductor

2761 **debussy prelude a l'apres-midi d'un faune and smetana the moldau**
recorded in february 1968 in the maison de la radio paris
orchestre national
charles munch, conductor
further issues: 523 (smetana), 2684 (smetana), 5211-5212
(smetana) and 6209 in set 6201-6212 (smetana)
cd: scribendum SC 012

beethoven die geschöpfe des prometheus, overture and adagio and borodin polovtsian dances
recorded between 6-14 february 1964 in the musikhalle hamburg
sinfonieorchester des norddeutschen rundfunks
pierre monteux, conductor
further issues: 503 (beethoven), 505 (borodin), 5219-5220
(borodin), 6207 in set 6201-6212 (borodin) and turnabout
TV 34668 (borodin)
cd: scribendum SC 013 (beethoven adagio and borodin)

2762 see 2688
2763 see 2585
2764 see 2542
2765 see 2242

2766 **mozart violin concerti nos 2 k211 and 4 k218**
collegium academicum geneva
armin jordan, conductor
franco gulli, violin

2768 **sullivan the mikado, scenes**
recorded in zürich
opera society orchestra and chorus
boris mersson, conductor
constance cuceau and marilyn zschau, sopranos
susan wild, mezzo-soprano
richard van vrooman, tenor
andrew foldi, baritone

2771 **britten simple symphony and respighi third suite of ancient airs and dances**
bulgarian chamber orchestra
athanase margaritov, conductor

2779-2781 (3-lp) scenes from operas by rossini
orchestre national de monte carlo
reynaldo giovaninetti, conductor
collegium academicum geneva
robert dunand, conductor
further issue: in 6-lp set of rossini opera
scenes from il signor bruschino taken from complete recording already
published on 2724

2782 dvorak symphony no 8 in g
international youth festival orchestra
walter susskind, conductor
further issue: in 6-lp set but retaining same catalogue number

2783 dvorak string quartet in f op 95 "american" and borodin string quartet no 2
quatuor de geneve
further issue: 3079 (dvorak)

2784 trumpet concerti by haydn, fasch, clarke, purcell and leopold mozart
collegium academicum geneva
robert dunand, conductor
roger delmotte, trumpet
further issues: 3074 (haydn), 5215-5216 (haydn and clarke)
and 5217-5218 (purcell)

2785 favourite melodies for violin and orchestra
collegium academicum geneva
boris mersson, conductor
christian ferras, violin
selections from the recording also on 5223-5224

2792 see CHS 1502

2794-2796 (3-lp) handel messiah
jerusalem chamber orchestra
scola cantorum oxford
mendi roden, conductor
cilla grossmeyer, soprano
linda hirst, contralto
frank whitmarsh, tenor
willy heparnas, bass
further issue: in 6-lp set of handel choral works but
retaining same catalogue number

2797-2798 (2-lp)   handel israel in egypt
israel symphony orchestra
scottish national chorus
john currie, conductor
patrice mcmahon, soprano
linda finnie, contralto
neil mackie, tenor
stephen roberts and peter morrison, baritones
further issue: in 6-lp set of handel choral works but retaining
same catalogue number

2800-2801 (2-lp) works by mahler
symphony no 5
recorded between 23-25 november 1971 in the salle garnier monte carlo

orchestre national de monte carlo
antonio de almeida, conductor
further issue: festival classique FC 60009
kindertotenlieder see 2442

2807	see CHS 1184	**2808**	see 168
2813	see 2400	**2814**	see 149 and 161

2815   brahms violin concerto in d op 77
recorded in the salle garnier monte carlo
orchestre national de monte carlo
david josefowitz, conductor
tomotada soh, violin
further issue: in 6-lp set but retaining same catalogue number

2816   ravel the two piano concerti

recorded in the salle garnier monte carlo
orchestre national de monte carlo
pierre colombo, conductor
lenore mila, piano
ritual fire dance
leonore mila, piano

2825   see CHS 1303

2826   christmas at the vatican
sistine chapel choir

2827-2828   recital of music for guitar
john williams, guitar

2830   **shostakovich symphony no 5 in d**/everest recording
recorded on 1 october 1958 in new york
new york philharmonic
leopold stokowski, conductor
everest issues: LPBR 6010 and SDBR 3010
other issues: world records T 281 and ST 281
cd: everest EVC 9020, priceless D 23697 and philips (usa) 422 3062
orchestra described on this recording as stadium symphony orchestra

2831   **khachaturian gayaneh, suite from the ballet**/everest recording
recorded on 2 november 1959 in the town hall walthamstow
london symphony orchestra
anatole fistoulari, conductor
everest issues: LPBR 6052 and SDBR 3052
other issues: in 12-lp set of ballet music, world records CM 41 and
SCM 41
cd: everest EVC 9020 and priceless D 22654
excerpts from the recording also on 5219-5220

2832   **strauss till eulenspiegels lustige streiche, don juan and dance
of the seven veils from salome**/everest recording
recorded on 12 october 1958 in new york
new york philharmonic
leopold stokowski, conductor
everest issues: LPBR 6023 and SDBR 3023
other issues: world records T 108, ST 108 and PE 751 and
sine qua non SQN 7115
cd: everest EVC 9004, priceless D 1323X, bescol CD 538 and virtuoso 3602
orchestra described on this recording as stadium symphony orchestra

2833   **strauss ein heldenleben**/everest recording
recorded on 1-2 june 1959 in the town hall walthamstow
london symphony orchestra
leopold ludwig, conductor
everest issues: LPBR 6038 and SDBR 3038
other issues: world records TP 165 and STP 165 and top rank BUY 003
cd: everest EVC 9033

2834 (2-lp) mahler symphony no 9 in d/everest recording
recorded between 17-20 november 1959 in the town hall walthamstow

london symphony orchestra
leopold ludwig, conductor
everest issues: LPBR 6050, SDBR 3050 and SDBR 3359
other issues: world records CM 16-17 and SCM 16-17
cd: everest EVC 9059

2841-2842 (2-lp) beethoven: opferlied, meeresstille glückliche fahrt, cantata on the death of joseph II and music from die ruinen von athen
recorded in the salle garnier monte carlo
orchestre national de monte carlo
zürich opera chorus
david josefowitz and boris mersson, conductors
costanza cuccaro, soprano
andrew foldi, baritone

2843 paganini string trios nos 4 and 5
tomotada soh, violin
claude starck, cello
dagoberto linhares, guitar

2844 concerti by mendelssohn
violin concerto in d minor
recorded in the salle garnier monte carlo
orchestre national de monte carlo
david josefowitz, conductor
tomotada soh, violin
concerto for violin, piano and strings
collegium academicum geneva
robert dunand, conductor
tomotada soh, violin
william nabore, piano

2845 concert from the 1972 international youth festival: dvorak carnival overture, rachmaninov paganini rhapsody and chopin nocturnes op 27 no 2 and op 62 no 1
international youth festival orchestra
walter susskind, conductor
peter katin, piano

2846 see 2079

2852-2853 (2-lp) handel belshazar
collegium academicum geneva
pierre andre gaillard, conductor

2852-2853 (2-lp)   handel johannes-passion

israel symphony orchestra
john currie singers
david josefowitz, conductor
patricia mcmahon, kirsteen grant and kathrin graf, sopranos
sheila lang, contralto
neil mackie and clifford hughes, tenors
stephen roberts, baritone
further issue: in 6-lp set of handel choral music but retaining
same catalogue number

2860-2861   see 2099

2862   recital of piano music by schumann and franck
jean fonda, piano

2863   beethoven mass in c op
collegium academicum geneva
pierre andre gaillard, conductor
kathrin graf, soprano
hanna schaer, contralto
olivier dufour, tenor
etienne betteron, bass

2864   works for guitar & orchestra by rodrigo & vivaldi
collegium academicum geneva
robert dunand, conductor
javier quevedo, guitar

2865   works for flute and guitar by handel and bach
marianne clement, flute
raul sanchez, guitar

2866   mozart organ sonatas
collegium academicum geneva
robert dunand, conductor
francois delor, organ
further issue: 3070

2867   choral works by josquin des pres
josquin choir
jeremy noble, conductor

2869   purcell music for the london theatre
accademia monteverdiana
denis stevens, conductor

2886   see CHS 1179 and 88

2889   mozart vesperae de dominica k321
collegium academicum geneva and chorus
david josefowitz, conductor
kathrin graf, soprano
barbara pressler, mezzo-soprano
olivier dufour, tenor
etienne battens, bass
further issue: 3071

2890   verdi otello, scenes from the opera
recorded in the salle garnier monte carlo
orchestre national et choeurs de monte carlo
david josefowitz, conductor
gerry de groot, soprano
barbara pressler, mezzo-soprano
stanley unruh, tenor
john modenos, bass

2891   concert galant au XVIII siecle
ensemble instrumental des concerts de paris

2892   beethoven piano sonatas nos 17, 26 and 30
nikita magaloff, piano
further issues: 6239 (no 17), 6241 (no 26) and 6242 (no 30)
6239, 6241 and 6242 comprised part of a set of the complete sonatas

2900-2901 (2-lp)   vivaldi juditha triumphans
collegium academicum geneva and chorus
robert dunand, conductor

2902   string quartets by mozart and schubert
orford string quartet

2903   choral works by liszt
ensemble alanda de geneve

2905   telemann paris quartets
quatuor baroque de la suisse romande

2906   concertini by pergolesi
orchestre baroque de paris
david josefowitz, conductor

2909	see 214 and 2062	**2910**	see 2088 and 2161
2911	see 2168	**2912**	see 2191

2915   mozart symphonies nos 5 k22, 11 k84 and 17 k129
camerata academica salzburg
rene klopfenstein, conductor

2916   see 2364

2918-2919 (2-lp) berlioz grande messe des morts/westminster
recording
recorded between 7-9 april 1958 in the eglise saint louis des invalides paris
orchestre et choeurs du theatre de l'opera
hermann scherchen, conductor
jean giraudeau, tenor
further issue: 6201 -6202 in set 6201-6212
westminster issues: XWN 2227 and WST 201
other issues: vega C30A 189-190, ades 21011, turnabout
THS 65017-65018, vox VUX 2013 and aurora AAB 104-105
cd: ades 14 0852

2920   see 2314 and 2406

2921 (2-lp)   massenet manon
recorded in 1974 in the salle garnier monte carlo
orchestre national et choeurs de monte carlo
jean laforge, conductor
yvonne bernard, soprano
michel marimpouy, tenor
michel cary, baritone
philippe desert, bass
further issues: 6318-6319 in set of french opera and festival
classique CFC 60008

2922   stravinsky music for two pianos
denise dupont and muriel slatkine, pianos

2923   tchaikovsky piano concerto no 2
recorded in the salle garnier monte carlo
orchestre national de monte carlo
david josefowitz, conductor
roberto szidon, piano

2924   see 2158

2925 donizetti l'elisir d'amore, scenes from the opera
prague chamber orchestra and chorus
ino savini, conductor
fulvia ciano, soprano
ferruccio tagliavini, tenor
gianni maffeo, baritone
giuseppe valdengo, bass
complete recording of the opera issued by supraphon and fabbri

2926 see 2157
2927 see 141

2930-2931 (2-lp) mozart die zauberflöte
recorded in 1974 in baden-baden
südwestdeutsche philharmonie und chor
david josefowitz, conductor
kathrin graf, anny may and inge weissenberger, sopranos
richard van vrooman, tenor
reinhold möser and rudolf hartmann, basses
further issue: 6326-6327 in set 6324-6330
excerpts from the recording also on 2949

2933-2935 (3-lp) mozart cosi fan tutte
recorded in 1974 in the salle garnier monte carlo
orchestre national de monte carlo
choeurs de l'opera de paris
pierre colombo, conductor
kari lövaas and enriquetta tarres, sopranos
rotraud hansmann, mezzo-soprano
erik geisen, tenor
klaus hirte and philippe huttenlocher, baritones
further issue: 6328-6330 in set 6324-6330

2937 piano music by bach-busoni, haydn and brahms
william trill, piano

2938 see 146 and 2119   **2939** see 172
2940-2941 see 2604   **2942** see 208 and 2139

2943 poulenc les biches and milhaud le train bleu
recorded in july 1972 in the salle garnier monte carlo
orchestre national de monte carlo
igor markevitch, conductor
further issues: 5227-5228, in 12-lp set of ballet music and varese
sarabande 81097
cd: scribendum SC 014

2944   see 2243
2945   see 2676

2946   **music for two harpsichords by krebs, couperin, tomkins and pasquier**
marinette extermann and anne gallet, harpsichords

2947   **mozart symphonies nos 1 k16, 4 k19, 10 k74 & 21 k134**
camerata academica salzburg
rene klopfenstein, conductor

2948   **cello concerti by saint-saens and schumann**
südwestdeutsche philharmonie
david josefowitz, conductor
kristy bjarnason, cello

2949   see 2930-2931
2950   see 2072

3000-3079 series: 12" lps containing material re-issued from the main concert hall catalogue
details included under each work's original issue number

5003   **symphonies by mozart, schubert & beethoven**
see 179, CHS 1257 and 2201
complimentary introductory lp for subscribers to concert hall's mail order scheme

5004-5009 and 5028-5029 symphony edition: eight 12" lps containing works by haydn, mozart, beethoven, schubert, mendelssohn, schumann, berlioz, brahms, franck, tchaikovsky and dvorak re-issued from the main concert hall catalogue
details included under each work's original issue number

5010-5022   de wereld van de opera/the world of opera: fourteen 12" lps containing operatic scenes, arias, overtures and preludes re-issued from the main concert hall catalogue
details included under each item's original issue number
this set appears to have been published only in the netherlands (muzikale meesterwerken serie nv), although the set examined has lp labels printed in german; some items may have been recorded especially for this album, as previous issue numbers cannot be traced (see details on page 191)

5030-5035 immortal symphonies: six 12" lps containing works by mozart, beethoven, schubert, mendelssohn, brahms, dvorak and tchaikovsky re-issued from the main concert hall catalogue

details included under each item's original issue number

5201-5228 immortal masterpieces of classical music

5201-5202 (2-lps) see 146, 2276, 2293, 2570, 2648 and 2663

5203-5204 (2-lps) see 209, 216, 2234, 2237 and 2537

5205-5206 (2-lps) see 211, 2470, 2471, 2514-2517, 2556 and 2742

5207-5208 (2-lps) see 2139, 2478, 2495 and 2682

5209-5210 (2-lps) see 2078, 2239, 2514-2517, 2579, 2598, 2676 and 2722

5211-5212 (2-lps) see 178, 2214, 2277, 2318, 2321, 2511, 2647, 2663 and 2761

5213-5214 (2-lps) see 182, 221, 2178, 2271, 2337, 2383, 2490 and 2648

5215-5216 (2-lps) see CHS 1254, 198, 2360, 2484, 2657 and 2784

5217-5218 (2-lps) see 2094, 2139, 2214, 2274, 2277 and 2784

5219-5220 (2-lps) see 10, 123, 221, 2189, 2233, 2252, 2279, 2536, 2761 and 2831

5221-5222 (2-lps) see 113, 2121, 2227, 2273, 2282, 2314, 2361, 2362, 2678, 2688 and 2744

5223-5224 (2-lps) see 2356 and 2784

5225-5226 (2-lps) see 225, 2095, 2147, 2168, 2214, 2217, 2218 and 2231

5227-5228 (2-lps) see 2943

6001-6013 the most beautiful music in the world volume one: 13-lp set

details included under each item's original issue number

6101-6113 the most beautiful music in the world volume two: 13-lp set

details included under each item's original issue number

6201-6212 the world's most beautiful classics volume one: 12-lp set

details included under each item's original issue number

beethoven bi-centenary edition 1970-1971: 66 lps in eleven sets

volume one: the nine symphonies and könig stephan overture
7 lps re-issued from the main concert hall catalogue and using original catalogue numbers
see 2275, 2283, 2313, 2332, 2400 and 2527

volume two: the five piano concerti, violin concerto and triple concerto
also including rondo in b flat, choral fantasy and piano sonata op 90
6 lps re-issued from the main concert hall catalogue and using original catalogue numbers
see CHS 1303 (2825), 2236, 2307, 2553, 2556 and 2598

6221-6226 volume three: the string quartets volume one 6 lps
recordings licensed from the fine arts string quartet and originally published on their own concert disc label

6221 string quartets no 1 op 18 no 1 and no 2 op 18 no 2
fine arts string quartet

6222 string quartets no 3 op 18 no 3 and no 4 op 18 no 4
see 2535

6223 string quartets no 5 op 18 no 5 and no 6 op 18 no 6
fine arts string quartet

6224 string quartet no 7 op 59 no 1
fine arts string quartet

6225 string quartets no 8 op 59 no 2 and no 9 op 59 no 3
fine arts string quartet

6226 string quartets no 10 op 74 and no 11 op 95
fine arts string quartet

6227-6232 volume four: the string quartets volume two 6 lps
recordings licensed from the fine arts string quartet and originally published on their own concert disc label

6227　string quartets no 12 op 127 and no 16 op 135
fine arts string quartet

6228　string quartet no 13 op 130 & grosse fuge op 133
fine arts string quartet

6229　string quartet no 14 op 131
fine arts string quartet

6230　string quartet no 15 op 132
fine arts string quartet

the three piano quartets op posth.
quartetto di roma
previously issued as 2652

6232　piano quartet in e flat op 16
quartetto di roma
string quintet in c op 29
quatuor pascal
walter gerhard, viola
string quintet previously issued as CHS 1214

volume five: the complete piano trios
also including variations on ich bin der schneider kakadu
5 lps re-issued from the main concert hall catalogue and using original catalogue numbers
see 2140, 2141, 2142, 2143 and 2144

volume six: the complete violin sonatas and cello sonatas
also including variations on ein mädchen oder weibchen and bei männern welche liebe fühlen
7 lps re-issued from the main concert hall catalogue and using original catalogue numbers
see 2702, 2703, 2704, 2705, 2706, 2707 and 2708

6233-6238   volume seven: the complete piano sonatas
volume one 6 lps

6233   piano sonata no 1 in f minor op 2 no 1
benjamin oren, piano
piano sonata no 2 in a op 2 no 2
nikita magaloff, piano
piano sonata no 3 in c op 2 no 3
alexander sellier, piano

6234   piano sonata no 4 in e flat op 7
alexander sellier, piano
piano sonatas no 5 in c minor op 10 no 1 and no 6 in f op 10 no 2
benjamin oren, piano

6235   piano sonatas no 7 in d op 10 no 3, no 9 in e op 14 no 1
and no 10 in g op 14 no 2
alexander sellier, piano

6236   piano sonata no 8 in c minor op 13 "pathetique" see 2221
piano sonatas no 14 in c sharp minor "moonlight" and no 23
in f minor op 57 "appassionata" see 2364

6237   piano sonata no 11 in b flat op 22
benjamin oren, piano
piano sonata no 22 in f op 54
nikita magaloff, piano
piano sonata no 12 in a flat op 26
alexander sellier, piano

6238   piano sonatas no 15 in d op 28 "pastoral" and
no 16 in g op 31 no 1
alexander sellier, piano

6239-6243 and 2709 volume eight: the complete piano sonatas volume two 6 lps

6239   piano sonata no 17 in d minor op 31 no 2 see 2892
piano sonata no 18 in e flat op 31 no 3
alexander sellier, piano
piano sonata no 19 in g minor op 49 no 1 see 2221

6240   piano sonata no 13 in e flat op 27 no 1
alexander sellier, piano
piano sonata no 20 in g op 49 no 2 see 2364
piano sonata no 21 in c op 53 "waldstein" see 2221

6241   piano sonata no 26 in e flat "les adieux" see 2892
piano sonata no 27 in e minor op 90 see 2307
piano sonata no 24 in f sharp op 78
nikita magaloff, piano
piano sonata no 28 in a op 101
alexander sellier, piano

6242   piano sonata no 30 in e op 109 see 2892
piano sonata no 29 in b flat op 106 "hammerklavier"
alexander sellier, piano

6243   piano sonata no 25 in g op 79
nikita magaloff, piano
**piano sonatas no 31 in a flat op 110 and no 32 in
c minor op 111**
alexander sellier, piano

2709   miscellaneous piano pieces see 2709

**volume nine: works for the stage   6 lps re-issued from the
main concert hall catalogue and using original issue numbers**
see 2120, 2274, 2540 and 2695
*2120 (fidelio) is actually re-numbered 6231 and also contains the overtures
leonore I and II listed on page 189*

**volume ten: choral music 6 lps re-issued from the main
concert hall catalogue and using original issue numbers**
see 2422, 2550, 2841-2842 and 2863

**6244-6249 volume eleven: miscellaneous works 6 lps,
comprising 2 lps of new material and 4 lps re-issued
from the main concert hall catalogue**

6244   musik zu einem ritterballett
orchester der wiener staatsoper
david josefowitz, conductor
further issues: 520 and 921
the two romances for violin and orchestra
orchester der wiener staatsoper
moshe atzmon, conductor
igor ozim, violin
twelve contretänze see 10

6245   see 2725
6246   see 2220
6247-6249   see 2737-2739

6270-6279   the world's most beautiful classics 10-lp set
details included under each item's original issue number

**opera series: eight albums each comprising 6 or 7 lps
re-issued from the main concert hall catalogue**

volume one: verdi la traviata, rigoletto and il trovatore
see 2227, 2371 and 2416

**volume two: rossini il barbiere di siviglia, la cenerentola,
il signor bruschino, le comte ory and l'italiana in algeri**
see 2688 and 2779-2781

6300-6305 volume three: bizet carmen and gounod faust
see 2184 and 2282

6306-6311   volume four: wagner die meistersinger von nürnberg and lohengrin
see 2029 and 2039
tristan und isolde, scenes from the music drama
recorded on 12 june 1973 in the alcatraz beausoleil monte carlo
orchestre national de monte carlo
geneva opera chorus
boris mersson, conductor
gerry de groot, soprano
barbara pressler, mezzo-soprano
stanley unruh and piero vezzani, tenors
ralph telasco, baritone
further issue: guilde 150.7050
selections from the recording also on editions atlas OPE-CD 1068

6312-6317   volume five: puccini madama butterfly, la boheme and tosca
see 141, 2286 and 2481

6318-6323   volume six: massenet manon and offenbach les contes d'hoffmann
see 2108 and 2921
gounod romeo et juliette
orchestre national et choeurs de monte carlo
jean laforge, conductor
yvonne bernard, soprano
michel marimpouy and romano pini, tenors
michel carey, baritone
alain pilard and philipe desert, basses

6324-6330   volume seven: mozart don giovanni, cosi fan tutte and die zauberflöte
see 2013, 2930-2931 and 2933-2935

6331-6336   volume eight: verdi aida, un ballo in maschera and otello
see 116, 2157 and 2890

6406-6429   the world of light music: brief extracts taken from the main concert hall catalogue

7020-7029   the world of light music: 10-lp set of brief extracts from the main concert hall catalogue
a further album numbered 7030-7039 was planned but may not have been issued

7120-7129   the world of operetta: 10-lp set of brief extracts from the main concert hall catalogue

*because of their fragmentary nature the extracts in albums 6406-6429,
7020-7029 and 7120-7129 are in most cases not mentioned in the
main discography*

appendix a: recordings whose first issue number could not be traced
*it is possible that some items were receiving their first publication in the
re-issue series*

mendelssohn violin concerto in e minor
sinfonieorchester des norddeutschen rundfunks
david josefowitz, conductor
saschko gawriloff, violin
further issues: 3066, 6106 in set 6101-6113 and 6204 in set 6201-6212

beethoven overtures leonore 1, 2 and 3
sinfonieorchester des norddeutschen rundfunks
carl bamberger, conductor
further issues: RG 130 (leonore 3), 944 (leonore 3) and
6231 (leonore 1 and 2)

debussy prelude a l'apres-midi d'un faune
orchestre des concerts de paris
louis martin, conductor
further issue: RG 119

appendix a/continued
borodin polovtsian dances from prince igor
utrecht symphony orchestra
paul hupperts, conductor
further issue: RG 112

rimsky-korsakov capriccio espagnol
recorded in april 1961 in bern during a visit to switzerland
halle orchestra
sir john barbirolli, conductor
further issue: 961

lortzing o sancta justitia/zar und zimmermann
orchester der oper frankfurt
georg walter, conductor
wilhelm strienz, bass
further issue: 5012 in set 5010-5022

bellini casta diva/norma
orchester der oper frankfurt
gianfranco rivoli, conductor
elena todeschi, soprano
further issue: 5014 in set 5010-5022

pergolesi sempre in contrasti; lo conosco/la serva padrona
tonhalle-orchester zürich
armin brunner, conductor
ruth rohner, soprano
franz lindauer, baritone
further issue: 5010 in set 5010-5022

donizetti una furtiva lagrima/l'elisir d'amore
orchester der wiener staatsoper
gianfranco rivoli, conductor
augusto vicentini, tenor
further issue: 5013 in set 5010-5022

verdi piangea cantando; ave maria/otello
orchestra della scala di milano
antonino votto, conductor
renata tebaldi, soprano
further issue: 5017 in set 5010-5022
this appears to be from a live recording of the opera which was
subsequently issued on various unofficial labels

appendix a/concluded

scenes from operas by purcell, donizetti, weber, wagner, massenet, humperdinck and puccini

tonhalle-orchester zürich

boris mersson, conductor

purcell when i am laid in earth/dido and aeneas

felicia weathers, soprano

further issue: 5010 in set 5010-5022

donizetti so anch'io la virtu; tornami a dir/don pasquale

reri grist, soprano

fritz peters, tenor

further issue: 5013 in set 5010-5022

weber nein länger trag' ich nicht; hier im ird'schen jammertal; kommt ein schlanker bursch gegangen; wie nahte mir der schlummer/der freischütz

elfriede pfleger and inge lentz, sopranos

fritz peter, tenor

theofried krug, bass

further issue: 5012 in set 5010-5022

wagner allmächt'ge jungfrau; o du mein holder abendstern/tannhäuser

evangeline noel, soprano

robert kerns, baritone

further issue: 5014 in set 5010-5022

wagner lausch geliebter; mild und leise/tristan und isolde

miriam kunz, soprano

fritz peter, tenor

further issue: 5015 in set 5010-5022

wagner winterstürme; hojotoho; leb wohl du kühnes herrliches kind/die walküre

evangeline noel, soprano

fritz peter, tenor

theofried krug, bass

further issue: 5015 in set 5010-5022

massenet je suis encore tout etoudie; en fermant les yeux/manon

felicia weathers, soprano

glade peterson, tenor

further issue: 5019 in set 5010-5022

humperdinck brüderchen komm tanz mit mir; ein männlein steht im walde; abends will ich schlafen gehn/hänsel und gretel

elfriede pfleger, soprano

gwyneth jones, mezzo-soprano

cd: house of opera (usa)

puccini bimba dagli occhi; un bel di/madama butterfly

felicia weathers, soprano

glade peterson, tenor

further issue: 5021 in set 5010-5022

appendix b: list of orchestras heard on concert hall records

amsterdam philharmonic society/see netherlands philharmonic
badische staatskapelle/opera orchestra based in karlsruhe
bolshoi theatre orchestra moscow
boyd neel chamber orchestra
broadway light opera orchestra/based in zürich
camerata academica salzburg
capella instrumentalis geneva and collegium academicum geneva
concert hall symphony and chamber orchestras/names used for
groups of players both in new york and in europe
crane university orchestra/based in new york university of potsdam
detroit symphony orchestra
frankfurter kammerorchester
geneva radio orchestra
gürzenich-orchester/opera orchestra based in cologne
halle orchestra manchester
hamburger kammerorchester
handel society orchestra/see netherlands philharmonic
houston symphony orchestra
international youth festival orchestra
israel symphony orchestra tel aviv
japan philharmonic orchestra tokyo
la jolla festival orchestra
paul kuentz chamber orchestra
lausanne symphony and chamber orchestras
leningrad philharmonic orchestra
little symphony and chamber orchestras/players based in new york
london philharmonic orchestra
london symphony orchestra
minneapolis symphony orchestra
moscow chamber orchestra
moscow radio orchestra/also known as ussr large radio orchestra
moscow youth symphony orchestra
mozarteum-orchester salzburg
musical masterpiece society orchestra/see netherlands philharmonic
netherlands philharmonic orchestra/players from dutch radio
ensembles, based in hilversum and also using the names amsterdam
philharmonic society and musical masterpiece society orchestra
new york philharmonic symphony orchestra/using the names
concert hall and stadium symphony orchestras
opera society orchestra/players based in new york
orchester der bayerischen staatsoper/opera orchestra based in munich
orchester der oper frankfurt/opera orchestra based in frankfurt
orchester der wiener staatsoper/players drawn from vienna's
staatsoper, volksoper and second-desk philharmoniker

appendix b/concluded

orchester des bayerischen rundfunks/radio orchestra based in munich
orchester des hessischen rundfunks/radio orchestra based in frankfurt
orchester des norddeutschen rundfunks/radio orchestra based in hamburg
orchester des süddeutschen rundfunks/radio orchestra based in stuttgart
orchester des südwestfunks/radio orchestra based in baden-baden
and also known as südwestdeutsche philharmonie
orchestra dell opera di roma
orchestra della rai di milano/radio orchestra based in milan
orchestra della rai di roma/radio orchestra based in rome
orchestra della rai di torino/radio orchestra based in turin
orchestra della societa di roma/based in rome
orchestra di scuola venezia/based in venice
orchestre baroque de paris
orchestre de chambre romand/based in geneva
orchestre des concerts colonne/based in paris
orchestre des concerts de paris/players drawn from the orchestre des
concerts du conservatoire
orchestre du theatre national de l'opera/opera orchestra based in paris
orchestre lamoureux paris
orchestre national de france/radio orchestra based in paris
orchestre national de monte carlo/opera orchestra based in monte carlo
orchestre pasdeloup paris
orchestre symphonique de paris
prague chamber orchestra
radio luxembourg orchestra
radio-sinfonie-orchester berlin/known later as deutsches sinfonieorchester berlin
ramat gan chamber orchestra/based in tel aviv
residentieorkest den haag
rochester chamber orchestra/based in new york
rotterdam philharmonic and chamber orchestras
sächsische staatskapelle dresden/opera and concert orchestra based in dresden
santa monica symphony orchestra/based in los angeles
schola cantorum basiliensis/based in basel
tonhalle-orchester zürich/opera and concert orchestra based in zürich
ussr large symphony orchestra/see moscow radio orchestra
utah symphony orchestra
utrecht symphony orchestra
west austrian radio orchestra
wiener kammerorcheser/based in vienna
wiener operettenensemble/based in vienna
wiener philharmoniker/see orchester der wiener staatsoper
wiener symphoniker/using the name vienna festival orchestra
winterthur symphony orchestra/players based mainly in zürich
zürich baroque ensemble
zürich radio orchestra

appendix c: index of conductors
numbers refer to the first issue of each recording

maurice abravanel/1903-1993
HDL 12

otto ackermann/1909-1960

CH-G6	CH-G10	CH-G11	CH-H3
CH-H4	CH-H5	CH-H6	CH-H16
CHS 1159	CHS 1163	CHS 1165	CHS 1166
CHS 1177	CHS 1178	CHS 1193	CHS 1194
CHS 1254	CHS 1256	CHS 1257	CHS 1259
CHS 1260	7	22	28
29	33	36	45
46	50	51	88
98	113	124	168
198	2014	2136	

antonio de almeida/1928-1997
2800-2801

moshe atzmon/born 1931

2551	2552	2553	2554
6244			

jean-marie auberson/born 1920

2356	2358	2360	2376
2381	2399	2410	2411

carl bamberger/1902-1987

CHS 1501	55	103	134D
141	145	147	148
152	155	166	177
179	2029	2039	2040
2052	2055	2065	2091
2093	2096	2099	2120
2135	2139	2147	

georg barati/1913-1996
2545

ernesto barbini/1907-1985
2157

sir john barbirolli/1899-1970
218   (961)

rudolf barshai/1924-2010
2272

arturo basile/1914-1968

2238	2259	2286

serge baudo/born 1927
2450   2488

franz bauer-theussl/1928-2010
2581   2591

appendix c/continued

paul belanger
CHS 1247

maurits van den berg/1898-1971

CH-G3	CH-H9	CH-H16	62
190	2002		

francois le berger

134F	135F

paul boepple/1896-1970

CHC 44	CHC 47	CHS 1107	CHS 1112
CHS 1231			

wilfried böttcher/born 1929

2484	2486	2487

pierre boulez/born 1925

2324	2379	2433

sir adrian boult/1889-1983

176	2103	2139	2161

fritz busch/1890-1951

CH-E1	CH-E13	CHC 61

pierre colombo/1914-2000

211	2179	2257	2593
2695	2816	2933-2935	

sergiu commissiona/1928-2005

2295	2296

pierre-michel le conte/born 1921

182	228	2094	2095
2107	2108	2119	2122
2168	2174	2184	2188

aaron copland/1900-1990
CH-F4

john currie/born 1934
2797-2798

clemens dahinden/born 1912

CH-E2	CH-E15	CH-F7	CH-F8
CH-F10	CH-F17	CH-F18	CH-G6
CH-G15	CH-H8	CH-H11	CHS 1064
CHS 1077	CHS 1082	CHS 1227	5
55	63	74	77
85	92	157	

pierre dervaux/1917-1992

178	182	203	217
221			

appendix c/continued

victor desarzens/1908-1986

CH-E6	CH-E14	CH-E17	CH-F2
CH-F8	CH-H11	CHS 1074	CHS 1106
CHS 1109	CHS 1128	CHS 1179	CHS 1253
57	198	2190	2191
2192	2327		

antal dorati/1906-1988

2300	2308	2309	2445
2446	2465		

robert dunand/born 1928

2514-2517	2650	2677	2694
2724	2742	2779-2781	2784
2844	2864	2866	2900-2901

piet van egmond/1912-1982
CHS 1255

jean entremont
2149

angelo ephrikian/1913-1982
2072

zoltan fekete/1909-1978
CHS 1065

edvard fendler/born 1902
CHC 21

anatole fistoulari/1907-1995
2831

lukas foss/1922-2009
2175

louis de froment/1921-1994
2577

pierre andre gaillard

2852-2853	2863

andre gallois

2199	2200	2228	2476

alexander gauk/1893-1963

CHS 1301	CHS 1303	CHS 1308

reynaldo giovaninetti/born 1932
2779-2781

max goberman/1911-1962
2292

appendix c/continued
walter goehr/1903-1960

CH-E8	CH-F5	CH-F6	CH-G1
CH-G2	CH-G7	CH-G9	CH-G12
CH-G13	CH-G14	CH-H1	CH-H2
CH-H4	CH-H8	CH-H9	HDL 1
HDL 2	HDL 3	HDL 14	HDL 18
CHS 1063	CHS 1067	CHS 1119	CHS 1121
CHS 1122	CHS 1125	CHS 1126	CHS 1127
CHS 1144	CHS 1153	CHS 1154	CHS 1158
CHS 1160	CHS 1167	CHS 1174	CHS 1176
CHS 1179	CHS 1180	CHS 1181	CHS 1184
CHS 1195	CHS 1197	CHS 1245	CHS 1258
CHS 1259	CHS 1405	CHS 1500	CHS 1501
1	4	5	6
9	10	12	13
14	16	17	24
25	27	34	40
43	54	58	60
64	66	76	81
91	93	94	95
96	97	111	120
123	125	126	127
129	130	138	146
149	153	159	161
188	192	197	216
225	2001	2003	2005
2008	2009	2010	2011
2022	2034	2038	2040
2052	2059	2067	2078
2079	2085	2089	2092
2100	2104	2105	2109
2146	2152	2153	2155
2156	2159	2166	2167
2172	2182	2183	2188
2201	2206	2209	2211

nicholas goldschmidt/1908-2004
142
nikolai golovanov/1891-1953

CHS 1302	CHS 1307	CHS 1309	114

vladimir golschmann/1893-1972
2212
tauno hannikainen/1896-1968
2559
richard haselbach
2299

appendix c/continued

hans hausdorfer
2063

gert heidger/born 1926

2134	2150

clifton helliwell/1907-1990
CHS 1110

fred hendrik
196

bernhard henking/1897-1988

CH-F12	HDL 16

heinrich hollreiser/1913-2006
CHS 1160

helen hosmer
CHS 1118

robert hull

HDL 13	CHS 1151	CHS 1189	CHS 1190
CHS 1229			

paul hupperts/1919-1999

CH-G5	CH-G13	CHS 1162	11
15	27	40	63
73	138	2064	

eliahu inbal/born 1936
2435

hiroyuki iwaki/1932-2006
2318

serge jaroff/1896-1985

CHS 1191	CHS 1192	CHS 1230	69

enrique jorda/1911-1996
2536

armin jordan/born 1932

2649	2766

david josefowitz/born 1918

190	2138	2164	2235
2272	2279	2315	2320
2407	2408	2440	2457
2460	2485	2550	2597
2664	2665	2676	2722
2744	2815	2841-2842	2844
2852-2853	2889	2890	2906
2923	2930-2931	2948	6244

appendix c/continued

joseph keilberth/1908-1968
2027

aram khachaturian/1903-1978
CHS 1300

boris khaikin/1904-1978
CHS 1317

paul kletzki/1900-1973

219	2233	2239	2241
2275	2313		

rene klopfenstein/1927-1984

2675	2915	2947

kyrill kondrashin/1914-1981

CHS 1312	CHS 1316	CHS 1318	2287

alexander krannhals/1908-1961

112	2033	2103	2121
2124	2148		

clemens krauss/1893-1954
2015

josef krips/1902-1974

208	2208	2216	2218
2224	2268	2271	2274

oskar kromer/1904-1949

CH-D5	CHC 33

jean laforge

2921	6318-6323

rene leibowitz/1913-1975

82	115	116	118
140			

jack lorij/1911-1999

HDL 17	HDL 19	HDL 20

leopold ludwig/1908-1979

2833	2834

lorin maazel/born 1930

2567	2570	2615	2626
2638	2710		

bruno maderna/1920-1973

2660	2661

athanas margaritov/born 1912
2771

peter mark
71

igor markevitch/1912-1983

2646	2647	2682	2943

appendix c/continued

louis martin/born 1907

146	2088

jean martinon/1910-1976

2612

brock mcelerhan

HDL 15

alexander melik-pashayev/1905-1964

CHS 1305

eddy mers

2363

boris mersson/born 1921

199	204	209	2232
2263	2345	2346	2347
2348	2350	2411	2448
2460	2476	2605	2655
2768	2785	2841-2842	6306-6311

alain milhaud

2305

darius milhaud/1892-1974

CH-B11

dimitri mitropoulos/1896-1960

2175

hans moltkau/born 1911

CH-E10	CHS 1113

pierre monteux/1875-1964

2332	2333	2357	2359
2361	2362	2761	

giuseppe morelli/born 1907

2074	2075

evgeny mravinsky/1903-1988

CHS 1313

hans müller-kray/1908-1969

117

charles munch/1891-1968

2494	2495	2511	2519
2527	2579	2761	

vassily nebolsin/1893-1958

CHS 1310

boyd neel/1905-1981

2097-2098	2166

ignace neumark/1888-1959

CHS 1237	73	2031

appendix c/continued
felix de nobel/1907-1981
CHS 1196
jeremy noble/born 1930
2867
karl oesterrreicher
2655
jack ossewarde
CHS 1131
willem van otterloo/1907-1978

227	2269	2276	2283
2395	2400	2406	2478

alberto paoletti/born 1905
2158
paul paray/1886-1979

207	2478	2648	2663

julius patzak/1898-1974
2106
anton paulik/1901-1975

2187	2383

bernhard paumgartner/1887-1971
2252
jean perisson/born 1924

150	160

pierre pernoud/born 1930
2423
blaise pidaux
2423
felix prohaska/1912-1987
2180
jacques rachmilovich/1873-1943

CH-AM	CH-AN

günther ramin/1898-1956

CHS 1234	2057

walter reinhart/1886-1975

CHC 59	CHC 60	CHS 1083

hugo rignold/1905-1976
2534
gianfranco rivoli/born 1921

192	2204	2205	2227
2234	2236	2237	2243
2250	2277	2282	2312
2371	2412		

mendi roden/1929-2009

2469	2470	2471	2653
2654	2794-2796		

maurice le roux/1923-1992

2490	2518

appendix c/continued

daniel saidenberg/1906-1997

CH-A3	CH-A4	CHC 22

kurt sanderling/born 1912

CHS 1316

nello santi/born 1931

2316	2416	2481	2537

sir malcolm sargent/1895-1967

2352	2538

ino savini/1904-1995

2925

ferruccio scaglia/born 1921

2169

edgar schenkman/born 1908

CH-A11

hermann scherchen/1891-1966

2918-2919

thomas scherman/born 1917

CH-E11	CH-F4

arthur schmittenbecher

167

carl schuricht/1880-1967

225	2214	2215	2217
2231	2246	2249	2258
2266	2284	2293	2321
2326	2378	2394	

alfredo simonetto

2238

nikolai sokoloff/1886-1965

CH-G4

henk spruit/1906-1998

CHS 1142	CHS 1155

abram stasevich/1907-1971

CHS 1304

denis stevens/1922-2004

2580	2659	2725	2869

leopold stokowski/1882-1977

2533	2602	2830	2832

robert stolz/1880-1975

2304

oscar straus/1870-1954

301	2302

josef suk/born 1929

2562

walter susskind/1913-1980

2782	2845

appendix c/concluded

hans swarowsky/1899-1975

2013	2030	2179	2186
2189	2307	2314	2317
2319	2322	2426	2439
2441	2482	2483	2542
2585			

henry swoboda/1897-1990

CH-AR	CH-C4	CH-C8	CH-C12
CH-D1	CH-D4	CH-D6	CH-D9
CH-D12	CH-D14	CH-D18	CH-E3
CH-E9	CH-E12	CH-E16	CH-F1
CH-F11	CH-F16	CHC 23	CHC 29
CHC 30	CHS 1073	CHS 1120	CHS 1135
CHS 1136	CHS 1137	CHS 1138	CHS 1139
CHS 1140	CHS 1141	CHS 1143	CHS 1258
H 1661	59	74	87

andre vandernoot/1927-1991

2240	2242

toon verheij/1894-1958

CHS 1162

christian voechting/born 1928

2270	2281

heinz wallberg/1923-2004

2410	2422	2442	2489
2540	2541	2586	2594
2595	2598	2604	

jiri waldhans/born 1923

2672

georg walter

135D	2102	2151	2202

hans-jürgen walther/born 1919

2101

john walther

149

lazer weiner

CHS 1103

august wenzinger/1905-1996

CH-H2

meinhard von zallinger/1897-1990

2026

alberto zedda/born 1928

2672	2673	2674

list of subscribers

production of these discographies would not have been possible without the loyal support over many years of

Richard Ames
Yoshihiro Asada
J.M. Blyth
Marc Bridle
Robert Dandois
Richard Dennis
Hans Peter Ebner
Nobuo Fukumoto
Philip Goodman
Johann Gratz
Tadashi Hasegawa
Ernest Johnson
Koji Kinoshita
J-F. Lambert
John Mallinson
Carlo Marinelli
Bruce Morrison
Alan Newcombe
Hugh Palmer
David Patmore
J.A. Payne
Tully Potter
Yutaka Sasaki
Robert Simmons
Michael Tanner
Nigel Wood
Ken Wyman

Stefano Angeloni
Reinier van Bevorvoorde
Michael Bral
Brian Capon
Dennis Davis
John Derry
Martin Elste
Brian Godfrey
Jean-Pierre Goossens
Alan Haine
Naoya Hirabayashi
Rodney Kempster
Detlef Kissmann
Graham Lilley
Douglas McIntosh
Philip Moores
William Moyle
Gregory Page-Turner
Laurence Pateman
John Pattrick
James Pearson
Klaus Reuther
Ingo Schwarz
Yoshihiko Suzuki
Urs Weber
Graeme Wright

Music and Books published by Travis & Emery Music Bookshop:

Anon.: Hymnarium Sarisburiense, cum Rubricis et Notis Musicis.

Anon.: Säcularfeier des Geburtstages von Ludwig van Beethoven

Agricola, Johann Friedrich from Tosi: Anleitung zur Singkunst.

Bach, C.P.E.: edited W. Emery: Nekrolog or Obituary Notice of J.S. Bach.

Bateson, Naomi Judith: Alcock of Salisbury

Bathe, William: A Briefe Introduction to the Skill of Song

Bax, Arnold: Symphony #5, Arranged for Piano Four Hands by Walter Emery

Burney, Charles: The Present State of Music in France and Italy

Burney, Charles: The Present State of Music in Germany, The Netherlands …

Burney, Charles: An Account of the Musical Performances ... Handel

Burney, Karl: Nachricht von Georg Friedrich Handel's Lebensumstanden.

Burns, Robert: The Caledonian Musical Museum ..The Best Scotch Songs. (1810)

Cobbett, W.W.: Cobbett's Cyclopedic Survey of Chamber Music. (2 vols.)

Corrette, Michel: Le Maitre de Clavecin

Crimp, Bryan: Dear Mr. Rosenthal … Dear Mr. Gaisberg …

Crimp, Bryan: Solo: The Biography of Solomon

Crotch, William: Substance of Several Courses of Lectures on Music

d'Indy, Vincent: Beethoven: Biographie Critique

d'Indy, Vincent: Beethoven: A Critical Biography

d'Indy, Vincent: César Franck (in French)

Fischhof, Joseph: Versuch einer Geschichte des Clavierbaues. (Faksimile 1853).

Frescobaldi, Girolamo: D'Arie Musicali per Cantarsi. Primo & Secondo Libro.

Geminiani, Francesco: The Art of Playing the Violin.

Handel; Purcell; Boyce; Geene et al: Calliope or English Harmony: Volume First.

Häuser: Musikalisches Lexikon. 2 vols in one.

Hawkins, John: A General History of the Science and Practice of Music (5 vols.)

Herbert-Caesari, Edgar: The Science and Sensations of Vocal Tone

Herbert-Caesari, Edgar: Vocal Truth

Hopkins, Antony: The Concertgoer's Companion - Bach to Haydn.

Hopkins, Antony: The Concertgoer's Companion – Holst to Webern.

Hopkins, Antony: Music All Around Me

Hopkins, Antony: Sounds of Music / Sounds of the Orchestra

Hopkins, Antony: Understanding Music

Hopkins, Edward and Rimboult, Edward: The Organ. Its History & Construction.

Hunt, John: - see separate list of discographies at the end of these titles

Isaacs, Lewis: Hänsel and Gretel. A Guide to Humperdinck's Opera.

Isaacs, Lewis: Königskinder (Royal Children) A Guide to Humperdinck's Opera.

Kastner: Manuel Général de Musique Militaire

Lacassagne, M. l'Abbé Joseph : Traité Général des élémens du Chant.

Lascelles (née Catley), Anne: The Life of Miss Anne Catley.

Mainwaring, John: Memoirs of the Life of the Late George Frederic Handel

Malcolm, Alexander: A Treaty of Music: Speculative, Practical and Historical

Marx, Adolph Bernhard: Die Kunst des Gesanges, Theoretisch-Practisch

May, Florence: The Life of Brahms

May, Florence: The Girlhood Of Clara Schumann: Clara Wieck And Her Time.

Mellers, Wilfrid: Angels of the Night: Popular Female Singers of Our Time

Mellers, Wilfrid: Bach and the Dance of God

Music and Books published by Travis & Emery Music Bookshop:

Mellers, Wilfrid: Beethoven and the Voice of God
Mellers, Wilfrid: Caliban Reborn - Renewal in Twentieth Century Music
Mellers, Wilfrid: Darker Shade of Pale, A Backdrop to Bob Dylan
Mellers, Wilfrid: François Couperin and the French Classical Tradition
Mellers, Wilfrid: Harmonious Meeting
Mellers, Wilfrid: Le Jardin Retrouvé, The Music of Frederic Mompou
Mellers, Wilfrid: Music and Society, England and the European Tradition
Mellers, Wilfrid: Music in a New Found Land: ... ... American Music
Mellers, Wilfrid: Romanticism and the Twentieth Century (from 1800)
Mellers, Wilfrid: The Masks of Orpheus: ...... the Story of European Music.
Mellers, Wilfrid: The Sonata Principle (from c. 1750)
Mellers, Wilfrid: Vaughan Williams and the Vision of Albion
Panchianio, Cattuffio: Rutzvanscad Il Giovine
Pearce, Charles: Sims Reeves, Fifty Years of Music in England.
Pettitt, Stephen: Philharmonia Orchestra: A Record of Achievement, 1948-1985
Pettitt, Stephen (ed. Hunt): Philharmonia Orchestra: Complete Discography 1945-1987
Playford, John: An Introduction to the Skill of Musick.
Purcell, Henry et al: Harmonia Sacra ... The First Book, (1726)
Purcell, Henry et al: Harmonia Sacra ... Book II (1726)
Quantz, Johann: Versuch einer Anweisung die Flöte trave rsiere zu spielen.
Rameau, Jean-Philippe: Code de Musique Pratique, ou Methodes.
Rameau, Jean-Philippe: Erreurs sur La Musique dans l'Encyclopédie
Rastall, Richard: The Notation of Western Music.
Rimbault, Edward: The Pianoforte, Its Origins, Progress, and Construction.
Rousseau, Jean Jacques: Dictionnaire de Musique
Rubinstein, Anton : Guide to the proper use of the Pianoforte Pedals.
Sainsbury, John S.: Dictionary of Musicians. (1825). 2 vols.
Serré de Rieux, Jean de : Les dons des Enfans de Latone
Simpson, Christopher: A Compendium of Practical Musick in Five Parts
Spohr, Louis: Autobiography
Spohr, Louis: Grand Violin School
Tans'ur, William: A New Musical Grammar; or The Harmonical Spectator
Terry, Charles Sanford: Bach's Chorals – Parts 1, 2 and 3.
Terry, Charles Sanford: John Christian Bach
Terry, Charles Sanford: J.S. Bach's Original Hymn-Tunes for Congregational Use.
Terry, Charles Sanford: Four-Part Chorals of J.S. Bach. (German & English)
Terry, Charles Sanford: Joh. Seb. Bach, Cantata Texts, Sacred and Secular.
Terry, Charles Sanford: The Origins of the Family of Bach Musicians.
Tosi, Pierfrancesco: Opinioni de' Cantori Antichi, e Moderni
Tosi, Pierfrancesco: Observations on the Florid Song.
Van der Straeten, Edmund: History of the Violoncello, The Viol da Gamba ...
Van der Straeten, Edmund: History of the Violin, Its Ancestors... (2 vols.)
Walther, J. G. [Waltern]: Musicalisches Lexikon [Musikalisches Lexicon]
Wagner, Richard: Beethoven (Leipzig 1870)
Wagner, Richard: Lebens-Bericht (Leipzig 1884)
Wagner, Richard: The Musaic of the Future (Translated by E. Dannreuther).
Zwirn, Gerald: Stranded Stories From The Operas

Discographies by John Hunt.

Mid-Century Conductors and More Viennese Singers: 10 Discographies: Karl Boehm, Victor De Sabata, Hans Knappertsbusch, Tullio Serafin, Clemens Krauss, Anton Dermota, Leonie Rysanek, Eberhard Waechter, Maria Reining, Erich Kunz.

More 20th Century Conductors: 7 Discographies: Eugen Jochum, Ferenc Fricsay, Carl Schuricht, Felix Weingartner, Josef Krips, Otto Klemperer, Erich Kleiber.

More Giants of the Keyboard: 5 Discographies: Claudio Arrau, Gyorgy Cziffra, Vladimir Horowitz, Dinu Lipatti, Artur Rubinstein.

More Musical Knights: 4 Discographies: Hamilton Harty, Charles Mackerras, Simon Rattle, John Pritchard.

Musical Knights: 6 Discographies: Henry Wood, Thomas Beecham, Adrian Boult, John Barbirolli, Reginald Goodall, Malcolm Sargent.

Philharmonic Autocrat 1: Discography of: Herbert Von Karajan [Third Edition]

Philharmonic Autocrat 2: Concert Register of Herbert Von Karajan Second Ed.

Philips Minigroove: Second Extended Version of the European Discography.

Pianists For The Connoisseur: 6 Discographies: Arturo Benedetti Michelangeli, Alfred Cortot, Alexis Weissenberg, Clifford Curzon, Solomon, Elly Ney.

Sächsische Staatskapelle Dresden: Complete Discography.

Singers of the Third Reich: 5 Discographies: Helge Roswaenge, Tiana Lemnitz, Franz Voelker, Maria Mueller, Max Lorenz.

Singers on the Yellow Label: 7 Discographies: Maria Stader, Elfriede Troetschel, Annelies Kupper, Wolfgang Windgassen, Ernst Haefliger, Josef Greindl, Kim Borg

Six Wagnerian Sopranos: 6 Discographies: Frieda Leider, Kirsten Flagstad, Astrid Varnay, Martha Moedl, Birgit Nilsson, Gwyneth Jones.

Sviatoslav Richter: Pianist of the Century: Discography.

Teachers and Pupils: 7 Discographies: Elisabeth Schwarzkopf, Maria Ivoguen, Maria Cebotari, Meta Seinemeyer, Ljuba Welitsch, Rita Streich, Erna Berger

Tenors in a Lyric Tradition: 3 Discographies: Peter Anders, Walther Ludwig, Fritz Wunderlich.

The Art of the Diva: 3 Discographies: Claudia Muzio, Maria Callas, Magda Olivero.

The Furtwaengler Sound Sixth Edition: Discography and Concert Listing.

The Great Dictators: 3 Discographies: Evgeny Mravinsky, Artur Rodzinski, Sergiu Celibidache.

The Lyric Baritone: 5 Discographies: Hans Reinmar, Gerhard Huesch, Josef Metternich, Hermann Uhde, Eberhard Waechter.

The Post-War German Tradition: 5 Discographies: Rudolf Kempe, Joseph Keilberth, Wolfgang Sawallisch, Rafael Kubelik, Andre Cluytens.

Wagner Im Festspielhaus: Discography of the Bayreuth Festival.

Wiener Philharmoniker 1 - Vienna Philharmonic and Vienna State Opera Orchestras: Discography Part 1 1905-1954.

Wiener Philharmoniker 2 - Vienna Philharmonic and Vienna State Opera Orchestras: Discography Part 2 1954-1989.

Available from: Travis & Emery at 17 Cecil Court, London, UK.
(+44) 20 7 240 2129. email on sales@travis-and-emery.com .
© Travis & Emery 2011

www.ingramcontent.com/pod-product-compliance
Lightning Source LLC
Chambersburg PA
CBHW071120280326
41935CB00010B/1067